KAI MÖLLER

TABLETOP DISTILLING

HOW TO MAKE
Spirits, Essences, and Essential Oils
WITH SMALL STILLS

Schiffer Publishing Ltd

4880 Lower Valley Road • Atglen, PA 19310 •

Type set in Univers LT Std

Photo credits: Unless indicated otherwise, all other pictures were kindly made available to the publishing house by the author.

The content of this book has been reviewed by the author and publisher to the best of their knowledge; however, they do not undertake to provide any guarantee. Any legal liability is excluded.

ISBN: 978-0-7643-5511-0
Printed in China
5 4 3 2

Published by Schiffer Publishing, Ltd.
4880 Lower Valley Road
Atglen, PA 19310
Phone: (610) 593-1777; Fax: (610) 593-2002
E-mail: Info@schifferbooks.com
Web: www.schifferbooks.com

For our complete selection of fine books on this and related subjects, please visit our website at www.schifferbooks.com.You may also write for a free catalog.

Schiffer Publishing's titles are available at special discounts for bulk purchases for sales promotions or premiums. Special editions, including personalized covers, corporate imprints, and excerpts, can be created in large quantities for special needs. For more information, contact the publisher.

We are always looking for people to write books on new and related subjects. If you have an idea for a book, please contact us at proposals@schifferbooks.com.

Contents

Foreword

Dear Distilling Enthusiasts!

I am delighted to write and publish this book, because it has long been my wish to show how wonderfully you can distill, despite the usually very strict legal restrictions on the private sector.

I thought I could write the book in a relaxed way during the winter months after Christmas, which are otherwise stress free for me, and was faced with the unwished for enormous task of writing this book in addition to my normal work, especially during the high season for my company and harvest time. Out of the wonderful "romantically idealized idea" of being able to write another book came some serious hard work under a fixed deadline.

Author Kai Möller

What a blessing it is, I thought, that I do not first have to try to find new recipe ideas, or to try out any specific functions of the individual stills. All the processes that come along with distilling are deeply rooted in my innermost core, and the contents I would like to convey have long been there. There is little else I do except dealing with the functions of stills and distilling. I just have to write down my knowledge, a time-intensive craft.

I need undisturbed peace for writing, which is not easy. Especially not for my environment! I would therefore like to start off by thanking my children, friends, co-workers, and my life partner for the understanding they have shown me. I hope this book will ultimately be an enrichment of knowledge and understanding for everyone, and at the same time something completely new in the market for books on this subject.

All books on the subject of distilling deal almost exclusively with distilling with large stills or using laboratory equipment. Even if the processes behind it are similar, the descriptions, recipes, and hazard warnings are difficult for most private individuals to understand. In Germany, Austria, and Switzerland, no one is allowed to experiment with large-scale distilling legally and just for fun! In most cases, already

Kai Möller brewing and tasting beer.

existing books describe commercial distilling, or in the English-speaking area, illegal distilling, so-called "moonshining." It has long been time for someone to write a new book on legal distilling of alcoholic spirits or schnapps. A book about distilling schnapps for leisurely enjoyment, for making essential oils as a hobby; to distill within the legal framework, just as you are allowed to in Germany or Austria privately at home, without coming into conflict with the law.

My dream—A book for enjoyment.

At this point I would like to mention the book by Bettina Malle and Helge Schmickl with the meaningful title *Schnapsbrennen als Hobby* (*Distilling Schnapps as a Hobby*). A great book with many recipes, pictures, and ideas which I would like to recommend as additional reading for my book, especially if you want exact recipes and quantities. Most descriptions and recipes fit well with the commercial two liter hobby and tabletop stills and the two liter limit permitted in Austria. As a second book, which deals specifically with legal hobby distilling, I would like to recommend the very well-researched *Handbuch für Hobby-Whiskybrenner* (*Handbook for Hobby Whiskey Distillers*) by Dirk Gasser. Above all, if you would like to make whiskey yourself, you can quickly attain notable results thanks to Mr. Gasser's attempts and the comprehensible descriptions.

With this book I would like to demonstrate what is described too briefly or is missing entirely in these two other books, namely how, despite legal restrictions, you can get really good and presentable results and everything that you can distill, including in Germany, and above all with the small 0.5 liter mini stills.

I have been experimenting for years in my UNICOBRES company, as well as out of my personal interest in my hobby, with the widest range of small stills and in the process tracked down several secrets. I can show you how to maximize yield, improve quality in home distilling, and still have fun doing it. One thing is guaranteed: In addition to all the laws and regulations that we have to observe, we still have a lot of fun doing things as hobbies. Especially if you replace the word "work" at the still with "fun" at the still, you will get success quickly. As soon as you begin to see distilling as a hobby, enjoyment starts not just with the later tasting and appreciation, but also in making your future homemade delicacies.

You never stop learning! Kai Möller in the Musée de l'Alambic museum, Saint Désirat, France.

Introduction

Can You Do Serious Work with a Mini Still?

Small tabletop and hobby stills are often barely taken seriously or are even ridiculed, but they work just as well as their big brothers. Each of the mini stills available on the market can really distill. This starts with the tiny "fun stills" made of glass of only a few hundred milliliters capacity, and end with perfect and fully equipped miniature stills, such as the new CopperGarden˙ whiskey still. They can distill everything. You can make any amount of different schnapps and spirits, aromatic hydrosols, distilled water, and even essential oils and fuels. And not just in theory!

You don't believe it? Then let this book surprise you. Every day I work professionally with the widest range of hobby stills and their owners, and can look back on many years of accumulated experience. In fact, some models exist only because I designed them together with the manufacturer and developed them further to perfection. The small Arabia stills with the integrated infusion strainer—possibly the best-selling small still worldwide today—would not exist without my development work. For decades, I have been working on barely anything besides distilling, and since I also live in Germany, increasingly with 0.5-liter miniature distillery systems. You may already realize that I have to observe the law in Germany and can distill only the permitted amount. Fortunately, even this works very well if, like me, you always make use of every conceivable accessory, or can use several different distillation models. Distilling with the mini stills works especially well if you know about everything you can put to use and the best way to do it. This is what I would like to show you with this book.

Let yourself be surprised! You can also distill on the smallest scale!

Distilling Is a Hobby, Not a Crime!

With this saying we have been trying for years to fight against the rigid German liquor monopoly and get a few things eased for us private distillers. Unfortunately, so far in vain. Up to now, as a private individual in Germany, you can work with a still with a maximum 0.5-liter volume boiler. This is unfortunately not very generous. Nevertheless, it is possible to obtain presentable, and even great results with a still of this size. Think perhaps about a typical chemical laboratory. The stills used there are seldom larger than those we may legally use in Germany or Austria.

NOTE | The stills that are used

In this book, I will mainly focus on the 0.5 liter size. Most photos show 0.5 liter systems, just as most of the recipes and experiences in this book originate from the world of mini stills permitted in Germany. Why should I make it easy for myself, if things are so difficult? If you live in Austria or Switzerland, you may think more generously and simply quadruple all quantities for results or ingredients. In Austria, you can work legally with stills with up to a two-liter boiler volume. Compared to German laws this is already generous! In Switzerland, you can even purchase and use stills with up to a three-liter volume without reporting it. However, the Swiss Alcohol Board limits the use to manufacturing essential oils, even though nobody checks them after you first bring the still home.

In this book we are distilling legally—no compromises.

Should the laws one day be relaxed in our favor, and if we are ever allowed to use five-liter stills, then after reading this book you will also be well prepared. The basics and principles of distilling are always the same, and it certainly does not hurt for even larger distillers to know the one or other trick to increase quantity or quality. If you have worked with a 0.5-liter still, then you will find it easy to come to grips with a five-liter still.

0.5 liter is the exception. Larger private stills are prohibited.

According to current German law, all stills up to and including five-liter boilers are to be regarded as private. So far no one can say how this will be handled in the future. Following the entry into force of the new Alcohol Excise Tax Act, authorizations for private small stills up to and including five liters can be granted by competent authorities. Unfortunately, it is currently unclear whether and to what extent such authorizations are to be granted and what conditions or requirements will have to be fulfilled. You will find more information on the current legal situation in the appendix. Initially, we are restricting ourselves to the 0.5-liter tabletop stills allowed at present to everyone in German-speaking countries. Austrians and Swiss simply quadruple the amounts, totals, and results.

What Can You Really Get Going with Such a Small Still?

I do not want to exaggerate, but you can make a whole lot of different things even with a very small still. To abbreviate somewhat and to provide more "clarity" right from the start, I begin by first explaining what cannot be distilled because the size is too small! This way, we can rule out any false ideas from the beginning.

What we cannot make in a mini still . . .

First, we eliminate any distillation of traditional and alternative fuel. We should not even try this with a miniature still. To produce gasoline, diesel, or ethanol of sufficient quantity and purity to be able to operate a vehicle is not possible with a mini still. I hope you do not misunderstand this. It is not impossible to produce high-percentage fuels yourself, but the result would be extremely modest in amount. The effort would not be worth it, not even for a miniature combustion engine such as those used in model vehicles. You would have to work an entire weekend to obtain maybe a liter in the end. This is not particularly effective. The fuel extracted would not be enough in terms of quantity to operate the boiler for the distillation. Distilling with a tabletop still is a hobby and should accordingly involve fun and successful experiences above everything else. However, it would probably be depressing in the long term if you put a lot of work into something that in the end yields hardly anything worth mentioning. If for private reasons you would like to experiment with alternative fuels or explore something specific this is certainly an exception, but not very interesting for most of us. Perhaps it would actually be necessary in some cases of application to leave the bureaucracy's desired "path of virtue" and emulate ancient alchemists or herbalists. Alchemists at that time occasionally had to carry out their research—which is still useful today—secretly, because otherwise they were accused of witchcraft and severely punished. It is still the same today, though for other reasons and with much milder penalties.

We have quickly landed in the region of alchemists and witches.

After fuel, I must confess that it would indeed be difficult to produce high proof alcohol or pure essential oils in larger quantities. But stop . . . we certainly are not giving up on this interesting topic. Difficult does not mean impossible, and just what are "larger quantities?" We are doing hobby distilling for fun and out of interest, so "larger" quantities are usually not necessary.

Beautiful miniature column still against an oriental background.

We rarely need more than a few drops of essential oils at home, and a bottle of lovingly pure home-distilled oil should suffice. These are quantities that we can produce with a 0.5-liter mini still.

For some more difficult products, such as whiskey or essential oils, we will fiddle with things a bit to make sure it is still fun and increase the amount somewhat. Basically, the solution is mostly simple and obvious. Everything is logical and fits together once you have dealt with the fundamentals. In the course of this book I will reveal a few small tricks to you that will help you achieve considerable success in all areas.

We fiddle with things a little so we do not miss out on the fun and success.

> **NOTE** | Example
>
> Did you know that essential rose oil is one of the most precious distillates and 1 ml—which is perhaps ten, a maximum of twenty drops—can cost around $60? The reason for this is that to make 1 ml of rose oil, you have to distill about five kilograms of delicate and freshly harvested rose petals! It is completely impossible to press this quantity into a 0.5-liter still and steam distill it! The petals would not even be properly dampened if you indeed wanted to try it. I can guarantee that you will never make real rose or jasmine petal oil with a 0.5-liter still! For this, you need a still with a hundred times bigger boiler.
>
> **But:** We still have the opportunity to easily make 300 ml of rose water in a single process out of the same raw materials, namely water and freshly harvested rose petals. Rose water is a famous luxury since ancient times and is much easier to manufacture. This we can do!

If we really do make pure essential oils ourselves, then we use plants with a higher oil content, such as cloves, lavender, or juniper. Just look on the Internet or in the catalog of a supplier to see which essential oils are expensive and which can be bought more reasonably. This will give you an idea of whether these are easy or difficult to distill. With a 0.5-liter column still you can certainly successfully make essential oils if you use the right plants and the right still. I have tried and tested this many times. But I will write more on this later.

With alcohol, it is somewhat more complicated to get into larger quantities. Above all, if the alcohol is to be distilled to a very high proof and purity, you have to distill several times in succession or have to rectify it intensely from the start. Here, only doing organized work helps. By using the correct method, you can fill one or the other flasks during the course of an afternoon or a weekend with a very high proof alcohol similar to the above mentioned fuels. In contrast, one liter of a 92% ABV is relatively a lot, as long as we do not use it to fuel a car, but rather process it further into liqueurs, alcohol macerations, remedies, or perfumes.

Kai Möller distilling in his recreational vehicle.

We can also produce special luxuries, such as our own whiskey, within the legal framework. My "hobby distiller colleague" Dirk Gasser has proven this and explains it in detail in *Handbuch für Hobby-Whiskybrenner* (*Handbook for the Hobby Whiskey Distiller*).

The most difficult thing about making your own whiskey is to stick to laws and traditions: by law, a whiskey must be aged for at least three years in an oak barrel. Traditionally it can also be aged for a longer period of time. The whiskey profits from this. This is where the actual result lies! Who would be able to leave their drink, laboriously manufactured in a mini still, to age for three or even twelve years in a small wooden cask? Apart from the "angels' share"—the share that evaporates into the air each year during aging—after twelve years the cask will have long been emptied just due to occasional tastings. Who could resist and would not try to taste their own drinks? However, there is certainly one good thing about all this: even if the cask might be empty at the end due to aging, you will then get into heaven, because you have already paid the entrance fee to the angels. In any case, this is what they claim in Scotland. The angels' share can amount to about half a liter per year in a small cask, so a two-liter cask would be empty after roughly four years.

The angel's share – or why whiskey distillers get into heaven.

This introduction is not yet the right place for these explanations. I will tell you about some tricks later, basically how you can reduce or even completely prevent the angels' share being taken from a small cask. I assure you, you can also make real whiskey with a mini still.

Making spirits is much easier and much more fruitful than distilling whiskey. Depending on the ingredients used, you can start at any time and get fantastic results within the shortest possible time, even with the smallest mini still. In distilling fine spirits, we hobby distillers find our true destiny. Here the tabletop stills quickly convince everyone with an enthusiasm for alcoholic delicacies. We have a lot of scope to distill either the tried and true, such as distilling the best quality Himbeergeist, or raspberry brandy, or gin—or to experience unique and unimaginable culinary delights with our own creations from the herb and spice rack. If the laws were not so strict, it would even be possible to be served with a still and accessories in a restaurant as a dessert and distill a delicious drink right at the table.

On the trail of the distillers—or how we can actually make up to ten liters of gin legally!

If hobby amounts seem too small for you, I would like to tell you it is definitely possible to obtain a significantly larger amount using a couple tricks. With gin everything is allowed, and we have the opportunity of producing up to ten liters of gin in a single afternoon legally with a mini still. Here we do not consider ourselves to be just "stillmen," but rather fine "distillers." A master liquor distiller can make a fine alcohol from his own mash, while the distiller extracts and mixes the individual aromas and conjures up special taste experiences. If we leave distilling of alcohol bases to actual master distillers and concentrate on making aromas with our legal mini stills, we can thus comfortably convert several liters of an inexpensive grain alcohol into fine gin and include it with professional gin distillers in terms of quality and aroma.

Conclusion

What remains guaranteed is the fun of doing it!

Unfortunately, it is not possible to do everything with a small still. What remains to us is a lot of fun, as well as an exciting hobby with enormous potential for discovering something new. An infinite number of possibilities remain open for the creative among us to enjoy their own culinary delights. Everyone else can access the already tried and true, and out of the huge stock of existing recipes and all their variations, they can stock their own home bar—as well as their medicine cabinet or cosmetics—with the best homemade quality.

The Stills

There is a relatively large selection of hobby-sized stills that are the maximum size permitted and can still be legally purchased. It really makes sense in the hobby area to look closely into the differences among individual stills. Depending on the application, the results of your attempts at distilling can vary greatly with different systems, especially because of the limited size of the mini stills, so it is all the more worth it to get the perfect still for the relevant purpose. In the legally restricted scale for a legal tabletop still you can only achieve the best results with the right equipment. For example, if you are thinking of making essential oils and high proof alcohol at the same time to create all the alcohol bases for your own perfume yourself, I recommend you start with two or even three different models.

Fortunately, the initial cost is not very high due to their small size. The prices of most mini stills range between $118–360, which is far below the level for comparably exciting hobbies. Even if you calculate in accessories, such as water tubes, pipettes, alcohol meters, containers, or small electric cook tops, the total expenses remain significantly lower than what you would have to spend for steam engines, tools, musical equipment, drones, or remote controlled model cars. And believe me, it is easier and more exciting in the long term to explore all the possibilities surrounding distilling than learning how to fly a remote controlled helicopter. You can equate distilling with flying a drone: these stabilize themselves in the air and thus make it possible to have fun and fly successfully from the very first day without expensive crash landings.

In This Chapter

- What Does This Hobby Cost?
- . . . Making Spirits
- . . . Fruit Schnapps and Brandy
- . . . Whiskey, Vodka, and Grain spirits
- . . . Essential Oils and Hydrosols

An inexpensive hobby thanks to relatively low initial costs.

What Does This Hobby Cost?

Making Spirits

To get started easily in this new hobby of "making spirits," you should get a still with an integrated steamer or infusion basket for steam distilling. Due to their higher structural complexity such stills are usually a little more expensive, but they are much more versatile in application. For example, the "Arabia" is still worth recommending, as it sometimes is available for just $176. I recommend a set of tubes, as well as a bowl with a cooling water pump as accessories. That would be about another $36 if you order the articles in a set. Besides these, a measuring glass and an alcohol meter are highly recommended, so that you can mix your own spirits to the correct alcohol strength. In addition, you need fruits and herbs from the spice rack or from nature, as well as a purchased alcohol as your base. You can use the leftovers from your home bar or buy inexpensive grain alcohol, brandy, or vodka. In discount stores you can get a bottle of cheap vodka for less than $9. Depending on whether you want to drink the spirit directly or would rather put it aside, you still need small schnapps bottles and possibly labels for labeling. If you would like to keep your results for later, it is a good idea to keep a book for your

Distilling with an infusion basket: versatile application possibilities.

A two-liter Arabia for making spirits.

records. In all, it does not amount to much altogether. If you are willing to spend between $236 and $300 at one time, then you are very well equipped to get started in the world of making spirits.

Fruit Schnapps and Brandy

To distill your own fruit schnapps, a simple alembic still is sufficient. Getting started in the world of fine liquors would theoretically be a bit less expensive than making the above-described spirits, were it not for the problem of obtaining the alcohol base. If you want to make things easy, it is enough to distill a purchased fruit wine. A cherry wine is sure to make a delicious cherry brandy, and this can be done without great effort; you can easily transform an apple wine into apple schnapps. It is the supreme discipline, however, to mash your own fruit and thus also make the alcohol you first need yourself. In this case, you will need various fermentation containers—a twenty- to thirty-liter size is ideal. Appropriate containers with accessories such as lids, stoppers, and fermentation locks cost between $35 and $48 a piece. The best thing is to have several on hand to mash different fruits to experiment with later. In addition, you need pH measuring strips, acid, yeast, yeast nutrients, and possibly a must scale. This can quickly become a few more dollars. In all, it is possible to get started distilling fruit schnapps, including making your own mashes and all necessary accessories, starting from about $350.

A simple alembic still—the classic for 500 years.

Whiskey, Vodka, and Grain Spirits

To make your own grain or potato schnapps, you need at least one good thermometer and a large pot in addition to the accessories described for fruit schnapps. The ingredients used contain starches, and we must first convert these into sugars with enzymes before we can ferment them. The mash must be stirred at two different temperatures, each time for a longer period of time. With a large pot, you can turn off the heat when the required temperature is reached and try to keep the mixture at the appropriate temperature using insulation or by timely reheating. You can do this more easily with a preserving kettle with a built-in thermostat, which you can buy for less than $236 and can maintain the temperature at the right level automatically. Anyone who takes distilling grain or potato schnapps seriously will sooner or later purchase a brewing machine like the *Braumeister* (Brewmaster) from Speidel. You can program the individual steps and temperatures into the brewing machine, and subsequent lautering and filtering the mash is also made significantly easier. Unfortunately, such a device costs well over $1,700, depending

Unfortunately somewhat more elaborate: making whiskey, vodka, and grain spirits.

on the size and equipment. If you consider that you can also make your own beer, buying one quickly pays for itself. Anyone who can brew beer can also distill whiskey, because the basic processes of mashing and distilling are the same.

Essential Oils and Hydrosols

For distilling essential oils, it is best to use a still with a large vapor chamber.

For making essential oils—like making spirits described above—you should use a still with an infusion basket or the largest vapor chamber possible, meaning the bigger the vapor chamber, the more productive your distillation is. You can get an appropriate still for less than $180, but for this you also need a cooling water accessory set with a small pump, because a good condensing system is relatively important for distilling essential oils to increase yield and quality. We also recommend a collection of small bottles or test tubes, as well as a few pipettes and a narrow measuring glass, so that you can cut the oils from the hydrosol and store them. You would be well-equipped spending $236 to get started.

Legal whiskey still with accessories.

The Art of Distilling

Before we begin to review the individual stills on the market, we should first familiarize ourselves with the theory of distillation so you can easily recognize the differences among individual stills and understand the connections correctly. I say, "First get informed, then distill."

If you are holding this book in your hands, you are already in the process of informing yourself. If you already own a still this is very good, but please read this chapter anyway. Even if you unexpectedly received a still as a gift and will certainly not buy a second one, the information from this book in its entirety will make you a master with the still. Ultimately, it is not the many individual technical aspects that create a "comprehensive whole," rather basic understanding that ultimately leads to success.

A great desire is fulfilled: a still under the Christmas tree.

23

The Basic Principle

You should know these basics . . .

We should first internalize an important basic principle before venturing on to doing our own distilling or buying a still. The theory is very easy to understand and valid for small hobby stills.

IMPORTANT	The basics

The more difficult it is for vapor to get from the boiler to the condenser, the purer, higher proof, but also weaker in aroma the result will be. Hence, the easier it is for the vapor to get to the condenser and to re-condense on its cold surface the more aromatic, but lower proof, the result will become.

Of fine aromas and stubborn mules . . .

Imagine aromas simply as something heavy that must be transported upward; for example, like a basket full of sand and pebbles. If you now imagine the vapor as a caravan of stubborn mules and obstinate camels, it soon becomes clear that most pebbles will arrive at the destination undamaged along a straight, short route, while a greater portion will be lost along a bumpy route through the mountains, and will have trickled out from the roughly woven baskets before the goal is reached. For this reason, there are stills with an extremely short and straight route, for example, if the condenser is set directly above the boiler. But we also know the opposite, namely the systems equipped with high columns or complicated shaped lyn arms and heads. In an extreme case, the columns are filled with so-called raschig rings or small stainless steel plates so the vapor "shakes off" the last bit of aroma before it is allowed to re-condense. In these, the camels would have to make complicated jumps over obstacles and climb steep passages before they arrive at the top.

If you keep this basic principle in mind when buying a still and know what you want to make then it should be easy to obtain the perfect distillery for your purpose. It is only logical that you would try when making homemade plum schnapps to "pilot" as much as possible of the fine flavor of the lovingly mashed fruits into the finished drink, and would like to use a rather "uncomplicated" still here. On the other hand, for a clear vodka you would rather try to get the vapor to divest itself of as many secondary aromas as possible on the way to the condenser. To do this, a still with a so-called dephlegmator[1] would be more suitable for "shaking off" the aromas and heavier components of the mash.

With the right still, you will be able to quickly achieve excellent results even just as a hobby. Distilling will make things more fun for you. The results will taste wonderful and do you good. Beyond this, whenever you use (or even see) something you distilled yourself, you will be happy remembering the feeling when you made the product. Over the course of time you will build up an impressive collection of hydrosols, essential oils, and various delicious alcoholic home specialties, and perhaps even discover new, unique fragrance or beverage compositions.

Steam Distillation?

You should also consider beforehand whether you want to distill using steam.

With a still of simple design, without a vapor chamber, you can produce wonderful hydrosols (herbal distillates), as well as most fine liquors (whiskey, brandy, fruit schnapps, etc.).

If you decide on a still with a vapor chamber, you can also distill all kinds of fine spirits (gin, *Himbeergeist*, hazelnut spirits, etc.) and certain essential oils (lavender, peppermint). In most cases, the vapor chamber does no harm if you just want to distill this way, while you really cannot expand a still without a vapor chamber or infusion basket later. In general, I would advise in most cases to get a still with a column or infusion basket because of the much more versatile application possibilities. If you are sure you want to make "only" whiskeys or fruit schnapps, a simple alembic or a whiskey still would be the best choice. If you tend to play with spices and herbs and would rather be understood as a *Destillateur* (distiller) than a liquor *Brenner* (burner) then a still with a vapor chamber would be the better choice. But more about that later.

---

[1] Due to the small amounts in the 0.5-liter range there will be very few systems with dephlegmators or rectifiers.

A large infusion basket in a two-liter "pot still."

25

Do you already know what you want to distill?

You should know in advance what you would like to distill and choose the right model still accordingly. It is difficult to distill high proof alcohol using a still with a short route for the vapor, and you cannot make any essential oils in a tall or a reflux still, which intensely rectifies the alcohol. With a still that is sufficiently large you can improvise relatively easily, such as cooling the swan neck (or even heating it), or subsequently hanging an improvised infusion basket in the still for steam distillation. It is hard to do this with small stills, so the system should be perfectly suited to you and your ideas right from the start. With an optimal design adapted to the later goal you can not get any better results from hobby distilling. Theoretically, all stills are equally suitable for making alcohol. This is why owning any kind of system is equally regulated by the authorities. As an ambitious hobby distiller, it could quickly become worthwhile to get a second or even third still for experimentation and determine the differences among your results.

I will now explain the different stills and designs that I have been able to find on the market.

A wide range of mini stills—which is the right one?

Buyer's Guide

First of all, we distinguish between the freestanding mini stills and stills completely equipped with stand and burner. You can see how many different models and versions of stills there may be from the photo on the previous page (p. 26).

Freestanding Mini Stills

Freestanding mini stills correspond to their big brothers in detail, because they are used in professional distilleries and commercial enterprises. They can be set up freely and flexibly in any location and can be operated over a fire, electric burner, spirit lamp, or gas burner. When buying a freestanding still, you should be aware that you will need additional accessories before you can start operating it. Make sure you think a bit about where you want to operate the still and how you will heat the boiler.

You have to improvise a bit setting it up, such as building a suitable stand for the condenser or the still. As a rule, the still boiler and condenser stand at the same height. While this looks highly decorative on a shelf, it is not an advantage when distilling. Remember, the boiler must be heated somehow. As a rule, it will stand significantly higher if it is

A freestanding 0.5-liter alembic still.   A 0.5-liter alembic still on a miniature cooktop. **27**

placed on an electric cooktop or other burner. You must compensate for this height on the other side with the condenser. It is best to always have a few wooden boards or tiles at hand to be able to set up your still safely and stably.

Furthermore, you want to be able to collect the distillate safely and not let it drip senselessly onto the table. To do this, it is usually necessary to construct the still even higher. It should at least be high enough that you can put a test tube, a measuring glass, or a bottle underneath it.

When distilling water or alcohol, you can also attach a tube to the outlet on the condenser and thus lead the distillate through the tube into a bottle. It works very well for me at home if I open a drawer in the kitchen cabinet and set the bottle on a board, like a "floor" beneath the work surface. Another practical solution is to distill from atop a counter onto a bar stool, or from atop a table onto a chair. Note that this method is only recommended for water or alcohol. When distilling essential oils, be absolutely sure to keep all tubes and pipes as short as possible, otherwise the small amounts of essential oils will remain stuck somewhere in the tubes and the yield will be much smaller. When distilling essential oils, you should set up your still much higher if possible, or have an appropriately large number of small containers ready to be able to trap the distillate. Alcohol and water can usually be distilled directly into a larger container, such as a bottle or measuring glass. Hydrosols can also be conveniently distilled directly into a larger container. If you want to make essential oils, then you should be careful to use a container that is as narrow as possible, leading to an even taller design. More on this in the chapter on essential oils.

Complete Stills

Stills that are usually completely equipped with burners and stands appear to be more practical and easy to set up, and can often be used right after they are unpacked. If you want to transform a wine into brandy or beer into schnapps, almost all tabletop stills will work well and can be used immediately. In the simplest case, simply plug the cooling water intake[2] at the bottom of the condenser with some chewing gum, a piece of cork, or some silicone, and fill the condenser with ice water. This is usually enough to be able to do a short and uncomplicated alcoholic distillation. In the worst case, just add a few ice cubes later by feel and let the hot water overflow from above using a short piece of tubing. This

Whiskey still in action.

---

[2] Pay attention to having the proper connections when purchasing a still. Some simple stills do not have a cooling water supply and you have to improvise. In any case, your still should have a cooling water overflow.

way, you do not need any complicated structures and can actually distill almost anywhere.

But if we expect more, then we run up against almost the same problems as we do with freestanding systems and must likewise improvise a bit. The problem with height is the same. Here, too, we have to extract the distillate either downward through a tube, or even construct the entire system higher up, perhaps on a stone or wooden block.

When setting up both versions, I recommend you think of an appropriate condenser from the start. It is quite possible to block the cooling water supply in individual stills and fill the condenser with ice water, but if you want to have everything perfect from the outset, you should connect it to a proper cooling circuit. For this you need a sink or bowl, tubes that fit, and a pump. Keep in mind that a 0.5-liter still barely weighs more than a pound, even with a filled kettle, while the long water-filled tubes will be easily movable by pressure and will try to press the still away from the burner. I have had very good experience using small clamps; this way, you can stabilize the "shakiest" construction with correct guidance by fastening the cooling tubes.

More about proper cooling and the optimal design of stills at the end of this chapter. Now, we will look at the widest range of models and their special properties to get a better sense of their forms and functions. In the picture below you see a sales room in Andorra. You can buy stills of any size there. At the same time, you can see how difficult it can be to choose the right system due to the gigantic selection.

The condenser with the connected cooling water tubes.

Do not let yourself be overwhelmed by the selection.

Stills and Distillery Systems
Alembic Still

The alembic still: a universally usable still for almost any purpose.

The alembic still (also alambic) is a traditional classic, and presumably, the most used basic design of all. Why should you change something that has been working optimally in most areas of application for more than 500 years? A real alembic is always made with a bubble shaped or round boiler, because this design distributes the temperature best over the entire contents. As a result, the mash is heated more uniformly, which is an advantage when cutting out any possible contaminants, but also prevents anything getting scorched when you are distilling "coarse" mash.

If you are thinking of making your own mash, you should choose this round boiler shape so nothing can get burned on. Also if you are distilling your own wine or fruit wines you should choose this shape, because the even increases in temperature in the boiler allow you to heat up any potential harmful substances in all parts of the mash, and later you can safely separate them.

A fully functional alembic mini still from the CopperGarden forge.

The third reason for a bubble- or pot-shaped boiler: tradition! Even in the largest distilleries, whiskey is traditionally distilled in an alembic still. If we peek into famous large distilleries, we will find traditional alembics of gigantic dimensions. As an example, I have received permission to print a picture from the Scottish Glenfiddich Distillery. There, in two big halls, stand ten large alembic stills, each 9,100 liters for the first distillation of the raw spirits, and another eighteen 4,500 liter units are heated by steam from underneath the floor. The basic shape of the boilers corresponds to our 18,000-time smaller 0.5-liter alembic stills.

Extremely large alembics in a modern whiskey distillery. *Courtesy Glenfiddich Distillery*

Above the round boiler there is usually an onion shaped head that first broadens out and then quickly becomes narrower, and is often beautifully shaped; it then tapers into a fine swan neck, and finally ends in a worm condenser.[3] Depending on the copper forge that made it the design may differ slightly, but the basic form of the round boiler with the "onion shaped" head remains the same in all alembic stills.

Thanks to this sophisticated design, during distillation the vapor can rise up through a relatively wide space directly over the boiler and carry along a lot of aromas with it. Alembic stills are therefore ideally suited for carrying along all the aromas contained in the mash. The distances the vapor travels remain short and the distillate can re-condense relatively quickly. Exactly the right still for all fine liquors, but also for making hydrosols, or for distilling the alcohol out of macerations, or from intensely aromatic spirits such as anise or caraway.

For centuries the matured and perfect design for every purpose.

NOTE | Suitability

To sum things up: An alembic is a wonderful still, above all to make fine liquors and hydrosols.

Due to its unique design for enhancing aroma, the alembic is not suitable for everything. If you want to distill an aroma-neutral alcohol—that is, very high proof—then you need a different still. With an alembic, traditional double distilling[4] is recommended for distilling fine liquors to obtain about 60%[5] ABV alcohol. No matter how often you distill, it will be difficult for you to obtain more than a maximum of 75% ABV using an alembic . Likewise, it is very hard to distill with steam using an

---

[3] Worm condenser (worm tub): Spiral shaped copper tube at the end of the swan neck in a kettle or barrel full of cold water.

Very high-proof distilling to more than seventy-five percent by volume requires a different still.

alembic, or to produce finer spirits or essential oils. Here also, a steam still with an especially large vapor chamber would be the better choice.

Whiskey Still

Essentially, whiskey stills, whether "wash stills" or "spirits stills,"[6] are identical to alembic stills. You can readily distill very good whiskey in normal alembic stills, as well as in special whiskey stills. The difference lies solely in the special shape of the head of the still, and I dare to doubt anyone can taste this difference afterward. Rather, this is due to the special touch, the individual style that a whiskey still is given by its special shape. Glenfiddich still has its own copper forge to take care of its stills and keep them in shape.

The whiskey still is also an alembic still.

There is a lot of emphasis on traditions in whiskey distilleries, so I would definitely recommend a whiskey still not only if you would like to specialize in whiskeys. Just as you can distill whiskeys with an alembic still, whiskey stills also work well for making fruit schnapps or brandies.

As a small special item, I would like to point out the new Copper-Garden® whiskey still. Like the large commercial stills, the Copper-Garden® whiskey still has an additional filling opening in the boiler, providing a great advantage over most other legal tabletop stills. This makes the still bigger! In Germany, customs allows only 0.5-liter boilers. This does not measure what you can actually distill, but rather how large the filling capacity of the boiler is, up to overflowing. Thus, in a normal still you can never distill 0.5 liters—but you can in a still with the additional opening. The still measures, as customs requires, 0.5 liters to the overflow of the opening. This gives you the opportunity to actually distill 0.5 liters with tightly closed screw fittings, which is also recommended for whiskey due to the rather low alcohol percentages in the initial mash.

"Charentais" Cognac Still

After the special whiskey still, you cannot omit a French-designed cognac or brandy still. Strictly speaking, the Charentais still—named after the

---

[4] Raw spirit and fine spirits: Distill the first raw spirit (the low wine) two or three times and collect the distillate for a final distillation of the fine spirit (high wine or heart) while removing the harmful contaminants.

[5] With a 60% ABV distillate you have the optimal mixture of purity and aroma. Later it is mixed with water to about 40% ABV drinking strength.

[6] In German, we would say *Raubrand* (raw spirit; low wine) or *Feinbrand* (fine spirit; heart or high wine) distillation. In the whiskey distillery, these two steps are traditionally completed in two different stills.

Whiskey stills—the distilling "pot" is one floor lower and is heated by steam.
Copyright William Grant & Sons Ltd. *Courtesy Glenfiddich Distillery*

"Charente" district around the city of Cognac—is also an alembic. One serious difference (noted in the picture) is the Charentais has two kettles.

This has a small advantage, since the distillate is first condensed by the vapor passing through the middle vessel, which is also filled with wine. This makes it possible to cut foreshots somewhat more precisely, benefitting the aroma later on. At the same time, the contents in the middle boiler are preheated and can be gradually introduced into the distillation boiler. Thus, you have a larger boiler volume, which can definitely pay for itself in the small scale of the legal mini stills. If you want to get yourself a Charentais, pay attention to the new larger intake tap. In the old models with the small tap, there were often problems with the seal at the tap.

The Charentais still—a unique filigree-worked piece.

We know the Charentais still, with its second boiler, in all sizes—just as shown here in Christian Drouin's Calvados distillery.

For hobby distilling, the Charentais is above all a striking beauty, and would certainly be an ornament in any home. Due to the filigree design, it remains much more complicated for practical handling. I would recommend the Charentais only if you are seriously interested in cognacs and brandies, and therefore want to work in proper style with such a unit. The Charentais is ideal for distilling brandy from wine, but also for distilling apple schnapps from apple wine or other fruit schnapps from fruit wines. It does not always have to be cognac; in the large Charentais in the upper picture, the delicious Christian Drouin Calvados is being distilled.

Arabia Still

The Arabia: the best-selling still for good reason.

The Arabia is the best seller at Destillatio, and for good reason. Its unique design with its tall head retains all the advantages of the original alembic still, but the head can be filled completely with herbs or spices and secured with an infusion basket.

Thus, this still also works well for steam distillation. The Arabia is usually offered as a complete system, and is one of the most versatile yet uncomplicated stills on the market. If you need a purchase recommendation I would recommend this model in most cases, because it is very hard for you to do anything wrong while using it, and you can also distill quickly and efficiently as a beginner.

With the Arabia, you can produce almost every type of alcohol, and with a little improvisational talent, even distill high proof alcohol. Do you see the high head in the picture? You can also fill it with copper wool or raschig rings to obtain a distillate with a significantly higher alcohol content. Remember: The harder it is for the vapor to carry the aromatic materials through the head to the condenser, the more will be lost on the way. The head attachment for the Arabia still offers ample space for the "pebbles in the way" of the rising alcohol vapor so it can "shake off" everything that clings to it along the way. The Arabia offers a lot of potential if you want to go farther and experiment.

Thanks to the column set on top, the Arabia is very versatile.

Even in miniature, the Arabia still is a beautiful ornament that is fully functional.

My 0.5-liter Arabia.

The vapor chamber might be somewhat too narrow to achieve real success if you are making essential oils, but it is easily possible to make hydrosols or very small amounts of essential oils. If you want to concentrate mainly on producing essential oils then a real column still might be an even better choice. For everything else, you are well advised to get the Arabia.

The Column Still

Column stills are the most versatile and are suitable for nearly any purpose. Unfortunately, I do not know yet of any tabletop column still with stand and burner, but there are freestanding mini column stills that are mostly suitable for essential oils, but also work well for most other purposes. If you are playing with the idea of purchasing a freestanding still anyway, it is certainly a good choice.

The column still: a royal class still.

The still can also be operated without a column as a simple alembic, as described above. With the middle piece (the column), the unit is perfectly suited for steam distillation, or to distill high-proof neutral alcohols.

Due to the still's small size and its low weight, you should make an effort to set it up so nothing can wobble or fall during distilling. In my kitchen, I can install the cooling water tubes under a cast iron burner

The individual components of the column still are beautiful to see.

The column still: the dream of all hobby distillers.

grate on the stove so they will not move, and if necessary, clamp them to the spice rack on the wall. The still stands on the bread box; the condenser is setup at the right height with a wooden block and a few tiles; and the head is fastened and sealed off from the outside with a bit of Teflon tape. This way the whole system is easy to get at and convenient to run. If you are willing to take some care setting up your system before every distillation, the column still is certainly a good choice for you.

My favorite still in the kitchen.

The Alquitara

As a large still, the alquitara is very popular due to the short vapor route and can also be used in versatile ways. Traditionally, grappa is distilled in Portugal or Italy in an alquitara still. There are a large number of different designs on the market, with an equally large number of different names,[7] but they all have one thing in common: the condenser sits directly above the boiler.

The best thing is to imagine figuratively how the vapor rises and condenses just a few centimeters higher up on the cooled copper surface of the water-filled still head and is directly diverted to the side. There can hardly be a shorter vapor route, and the vapor can carry along aromas and other heavier components without any hindrance.

Very early on, people came up with the idea of hanging a cloth over the vessel, of installing an additional infusion basket, or, as with Helge Schmickl's Leonardo still, improvising with an additional steamer in the boiler as an infusion basket for distilling essential oils. In fact, the alquitara is optimally suited for making essential oils, even if the column stills promise greater yields due to their greater capacity in the vapor chamber. Resourceful craftsmen and commercial producers like to build their own columns between the alquitara's boiler and head attachment. In more tolerant countries, such as Austria or Switzerland, there are also legal two-liter or three-liter sizes—the so-called alquitara "plus," a combination of the alquitara and a column still.

0.5-liter alquitara still with spirit burner.

If you are lucky enough to be able to work with a two- or three-liter still, then an alquitara with a column for making essential oils would certainly be the best choice. According to current law as amended in Germany, we are limited to the 0.5-liter unit, and the vapor chamber of an alquitara still is too small. In addition, handling the extra baskets can be cumbersome in practice in some models.

---

[7] Alquitara, Alquitara Plus, Leonardo, and a "mushroom" shaped still.

Various alquitara
still models.

Modern equipped
hennin still with
infusion basket.

For these reasons I would only recommend a miniature alquitara for distilling simple brandies from wine or to complete your still collection. For practical distilling, or as a starter model, an alembic, Arabia, or a column still would certainly be the better choice, depending on your intended purpose.

Hennin Still

The hennin still from the CopperGarden® forge is another special item, and also works excellently for making hydrosols. Its special feature lies in the expandable steamer baskets that can be placed between the still's head and boiler and can be filled with herbs. In this way, it is possible to send the vapor through larger quantities of herbs, similarly to column stills.

As an additional feature there is a collector in the head that directs condensed distillate to the swan neck early on. Here again the vapor routes are extremely short, promising a high distillate quality and quantity, provided you succeed in cooling the head sufficiently well. This is the disadvantage of the hennin still! It is a historical still model from a time when air was used for condensation. The high, pointed head provides the potential to cool the vapor down sufficiently in a cold room or with water so that it condenses and drips down from the side spigot.

To get a really good quality and quantity of essential oils you need a much more intense condensation. In earlier times they laid damp cloths on the heads, which is not really useful on the small surface of the 0.5-liter version; the cloths heat up too quickly and must be changed constantly. I would recommend only distilling in winter and putting snow on the head, or spraying the head with a lot of cold water during distilling.

If you prefer to distill according to traditional alchemy, the hennin still is certainly a good choice. Even if you only want to produce hydrosols or distill in a cold environment you can choose this model. The hennin still really works well if you want to be able to understand the processes during distillation better as a "learning object" for trying out different condensation methods. In most cases, I would advise you to try another system.

The hennin still's infusion basket in detail.

Retorts, Glass Flasks, and Pelicans

The selection of glass stills is enormous; nevertheless, I would like to summarize all the glass devices, despite their differences. Historically, glass has always been used for distilling,[8] above all because you can watch it very well and thereby better understand what actually happens in a still. That is also the main reason I would advise you to get a glass system as a second or third still.

Glass devices are ideally suited for testing set ups and experiments.

There are a lot of smaller fun stills made of glass available on the market, such as the beautiful 300 ml system by thermometer manufacturer TFA Dostmann (see p. 41). Because of their small size and the material—which does not work very well for distilling alcohol—these models are only suitable for occasionally turning a glass of old wine into a brandy, perhaps for a circle of friends at the table. In the production of alcohol, copper is relatively important as a material. Copper can neutralize unpleasant tasting sulfuric acid that otherwise affects the aroma. For this reason, in the commercial sector alcohol is always distilled in pot stills with copper distillation heads. If you distill alcohol as a hobby, you should always use a copper still. Alternatively, if you prefer to distill in glass, a small trick helps.

---

[8] For example, even today in the authentic Prague alchemy laboratory "Spulum Alchemiae" you can still marvel at the adjacent underground "secret" glassblowing workshop from the sixteenth century.

Classic pelican still made of modern laboratory glass.

Complicated setup of glass devices for extracting aromas in the *Erichs Schnapsbrände* (Erich's schnapps distillery) museum in Germany's Black Forest.

To distill a higher proof, but also a more appetizing alcohol, fill the space above the glass flask—possibly a separate, attached small glass column—with copper wool and force the vapor through it.

A second reason for distilling in glass might also be its historical similarity to early alchemists. In addition to the fun of distilling as described above, I know several historical replicas of retorts and flasks, such as the 0.5-liter pelican still made of sturdy Duran˙ laboratory glass by Al-Ambik˙. Nowadays, these devices are fortunately made of modern and relatively unbreakable glass, and are ideal for observing the individual processes during distillation. If you want to distill for spiritual reasons and extract the "mind, body, and soul" from plants (or other materials) in your environment and join these together again[9] in a refined form as a healing essence, then the clear and easily comprehensible individual work steps in a beautifully shaped glass retort can definitely contribute; this also lets you experience some wisdom to recognize basic philosophical truths.

Last but not least, we still have the perfectly matched laboratory devices,[10] which unfortunately are usually very expensive and require appropriate accessories, such as special laboratory heaters or tripods. Above all, you can experiment with laboratory equipment and observe or measure everything very exactly. If you are interested in exact results and quantity units then laboratory equipment is your best choice. The standardized plug connections are also a great advantage. It is always possible to replace defective components at any time and eventually one day discover a large flask at a flea market that was overlooked by the authorities. At the same time, I will not conceal the many disadvantages. Apart from the costs and relatively high risk of breakage, it is difficult to clean a glass flask due to the narrow neck width. Especially when something gets scorched on it, often the only thing you can do is buy a new flask.

---

[9] The wisdom of the ancient alchemists: *Solve y Coagula*, "Breaking down and gathering together."

[10] The photo of the laboratory stills comes from the wonderful museum at Erichs *Schnapshäusle* (schnapps hut) in the Black Forest.

Rum Still

Another unique piece among 0.5-liter stills is the so-called rum still. Strictly speaking, these are the precursors of today's column stills, with the only difference being that the columns are not fastened above the boiler, but set to the side. The name is misleading, since these systems are still used today on a large scale in the Caribbean to distill rum, but we also find similar ones in Europe for distilling other alcohols, such as Armagnac. This, in contrast to cognac, is distilled in a single process, and therefore the columns are needed as a dephlegmator for higher proof distillation. From this point of view, you could also call this still an Armagnac or column still.

Multiple column distilleries were formerly gladly used in the industry.

When you look at the still and imagine how the vapor rises from the boiler, penetrates through the thin swan neck, and expands in the first column, where it is able to collect somewhat, just to flow again through a small swan neck and collect in another column before it finally enters the condenser, then you can imagine how few aromas the vapor has left in the end. In fact, distillation with columns is indeed designed to obtain alcohol of a sufficiently high proof in the first run. We should also be aware that this type of distillation system is under continuous operation in industrial distilleries; the boiler is always being refilled and continuously heated under constant operation. As a result, the columns also reach a consistently uniform temperature, helping guide the vapor to the condenser.

Large multi-column stills.

Things are a bit different with our model. We have a 0.5-liter boiler, and if something goes wrong, the evaporating liquid will condense in the columns before it reaches the condenser. This means that, depending on the alcohol content of the liquid to be distilled, the air pressure, and the external temperature, we may get almost no result at all at the end of the condenser. What we do get can be extremely high proof. For this, you obtain two more fractions from the still, which are collected in the side columns at different degrees of purity and in different amounts. An interesting game, especially if you like to experiment with alcohol percentages. It is also possible to heat the columns using a spirit burner or a basin of lighting gel to obtain a completely different result.

With all these possibilities, the "Caribbean" still from the Copper-Garden® forge is a uniquely versatile device for distilling alcohol which I would only recommend if you have already gained some experience using other systems.

Such a multi-column still works particularly well for experimenting with a second still.

Theoretically, the Caribbean would even be suitable for making essential oils. I know of a lot of column stills of a similar type on a large scale in which the columns are filled with plant material, and hot water vapor is steamed through them. In Portugal, grappa or marc is made this way on an industrial scale (on p. 42 is a large, mobile, three-column system[11]).

Tabletop Pot Still

In German usage[12] "pot still" refers mainly to home-built stills in which a normal pot serves as a boiler, but also to the many different stills on the market with a flat boiler. The selection and different shapes of tabletop stills is enormous. The Ferrari still (right) is characterized by its glass condenser; a quite interesting model, albeit unfortunately too big for a German user, since the boiler can hold a liter, and therefore it would only be allowed for Austrian or Swiss distillers. One drawback that almost all tabletop pot stills have is that the boiler size is generally larger than the 0.5 liters tolerated in Germany.

Beautiful miniature "crystal" still with glass condenser.

[11] The image comes from the Musée de l'Alambic—which is worth visiting—in Saint-Désirat, in southeastern France.

[12] In English, the name is also used for large whiskey stills.

Typical tabletop pot still for hobby distillers.

An exception is the 0.4-liter still shown, which also comes from Ferrari in Italy, but unfortunately is no longer available.

The "Classic" still by Helge Schmickl of Austria is relatively well-known; with its additional infusion basket made of stainless steel, it is also suitable for steam distillation. This is a tried and tested trick you can use with almost all pot stills with a boiler that is wide enough. You just need a steamer—you can find one in almost any houseware store—and three stainless steel screws to hold up the steamer when it is installed. Then you can fill the upper part of the boiler with plant material. Another advantage of the "Classic" is the replaceable boiler. With this design it would be possible to—illegally—buy the still in Austria in the legal two-liter size and later replace the kettle with a larger one.

"Classic" stills are very similar to the Italian "hobby" still by Ferrari or the Portuguese version, the "Hobby II," by CopperGarden˙ forge, which is also available for purchase in an electric version, in addition to the version with the spirit burner (see following). Both have the same functions and can be used for steam distillation with the infusion basket. The additional larger boiler is only available with the "Classic."

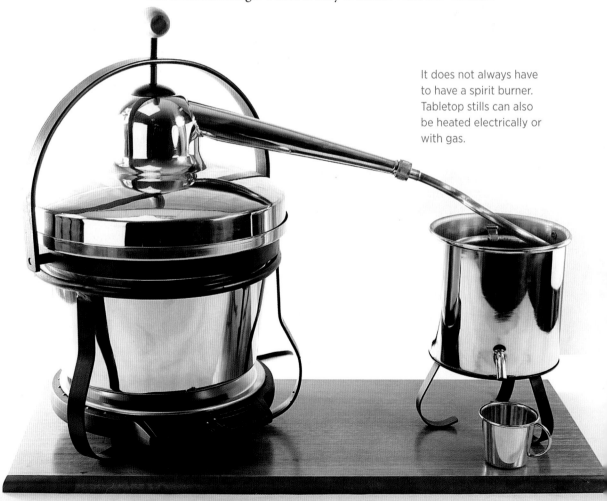

It does not always have to have a spirit burner. Tabletop stills can also be heated electrically or with gas.

Likewise very popular is the so-called "Italia" still, which comes with a copper infusion basket as standard equipment. Because of its tall, pointed head, the system is also sometimes called a "Tipi" or "tent still." Unfortunately, the still holds three liters and can therefore only be legally sold in Switzerland for distilling essential oils. Thanks to the infusion basket and the generous head you can distill very well using this still.

Water Distiller

Stills for making distilled water are generally prohibited in Germany because of their size. The volume is often four or five liters, and German customs has the view that it is also possible to distill alcohol using such a still, because, by all appearances, people sometimes do so in Sweden and Norway. I would advise against this. If possible, alcohol should always be distilled in copper, to neutralize sulfuric acid and obtain a smooth aroma. Despite strict German laws, some of these systems are sold by "ignorant" traders as normal kitchen appliances. This is what they were developed and built for. In the evening, water is poured into the boiler, the machine runs overnight, and by the next morning it delivers a container full of pure, distilled water freed of all contaminants. Due to the dealers' ignorance, it is relatively easy to find a suitable system in an electronics store or on the Internet and buy it without registering with the authorities.

Another lovely miniature still from my collection.

An electric water distiller as a kitchen appliance.

The Italian GAGGIA

If you are lucky, you might find an electric still made by well-known Italian coffee maker Gaggia at a flea market or on eBay.

The Gaggia still was an attempt in the 1970s to make distilling palatable to a broader mass market. Unfortunately, production was stopped for unknown reasons. Maybe the time was not yet ripe for such a fantastic product and sales were sluggish; perhaps it was also legislation, which is far more difficult to understand in international terms than a coffee machine manufacturer might want to attempt.

The Gaggia still, a two-liter copper boiler that is legal under Italian law, was electrically heated from underneath. A glass condenser fitted with tubes instead of a swan neck was supplied. The special features of the Gaggia still were the fittings and the really secure way it could be set up thanks to its solid substructure and the stand. The manufacturer also supplied an extremely useful manual with a good overview poster on how to produce aromas and essences for use in the kitchen, in cosmetics, and medicines. A truly unique still, and it is a pity that they no longer exist today.

Espresso Still

Since I just explained the Italian Gaggia still, what finally remains is the "normal" espresso still as we all know it. These involve exactly the many small "cafeteria" and espresso coffee makers that are also regarded as small stills. Here, water is heated in a boiler and then passed upward into a filter basket filled with coffee, but without cooling it, because we prefer our coffee hot. Actually, it is the same principle as an alquitara still. A silicone tube can be easily connected directly to the still and passed through a condenser. Then we have a still that would also be suitable for making alcohol. Strangely enough, customs allows the purchase of espresso machines even of larger dimensions.

This is what we use to distill coffee!

We can see this even more clearly in a Belgian coffee siphon. Here, the water is heated in a separate boiler and specifically directed through a swan neck into a glass containing coffee next to it. The highlight of this distillation is the ingenious mechanism by means of a counterweight. As soon as the boiler is empty, the weight lowers and lifts the light boiler. The burner beneath flips shut, the flame is extinguished, and due to the vacuum in the pot and the difference in height, the coffee begins to run back into the pot as if directed by a magical hand; you can then fill a cup with the freshly brewed coffee from the pot through a spigot. Unique.

Stills larger than a 0.5 liter must be reported. Does that also mean espresso distillers?

Setting Up a Still

I am always being asked what is the best way to set up a still. I have suffered for years from a certain blindness on the subject, because I assumed that there is logically only one possible way to construct a still. For me, setting one up was a simple routine, and I rarely had to think about it. Thanks to some particularly nice customers and many friends who took the trouble to describe their problems to me in more detail, I realized in time that a left-handed person would probably set up a still for practical work differently than a right-handed person. And something else: I set stills up out of habit from left to right. We write from left to right, a clock runs to the right (clockwise), and water currents revolve to the right, just like low pressure areas in the northern hemisphere of our planet. Presumably thanks to the cultural environment in which I grew up, it is logical for me and rooted in my inner being to distill from left to right. Technically there is no difference, and someone from another cultural background might prefer to distill from right to left.

A carton full of single items: Boiler, condenser, head, and swan neck? Should there be anything else?

If I look at a newly delivered miniature system through the eyes of my customers, I see a lot of different parts in a cardboard box with which I could not get very much going. If I spread out all the parts along with the accessory set in front of me, then I also realize that there is actually a lot to consider. In the worst case, any incorrect setup or lack of preparation for what is going to happen could even become dangerous. Especially with the miniature systems, we have to constantly improvise somewhere. Because of its "smallness," a legal still, with its sometimes tiny connections, cannot always be constructed as stably as it should be when dealing with excess pressure or with combustible materials. Setting up a still requires special attention for safety reasons alone. For this reason, we are now dealing first of all with the right way to construct our still.

All these parts are now lying in front of us. If we have already informed ourselves in advance or read this book carefully, we can certainly identify the boiler, the still head, and the condenser, and put these together properly. This is the easiest part, because there are not a great many possibilities for variance. Did your still come with a stand? Then it is certainly also easily possible for you to set the one (with some stills the two) stand(s) in the right place. The burner should also be clearly assigned to its place: no matter what burner you use, it should be under the boiler, not under the condenser.[13]

The basic components of any still.

We are now in the "dry run," because before we begin to distill seriously, we should have set the still up correctly at least once. Whenever you distill, it is best if you carefully go through the checklist on page 55. Just like a pilot checks his airplane before taking off for all points on his checklist, so you should also make it a habit, before filling or heating your still, to check how everything fits and whether you can work with your setup safely and sensibly. Especially as a beginner, you will easily overlook small things that are important in day-to-day operation.

A raised setup on wooden blocks during a distilling seminar.

---

[13] A little joke, but I actually have a picture from the video game *Far Cry* in which the burner of a still sits under the condenser and the distillation is done the wrong way.

Attention:
Explosive,
flammable, and
really hot!

IMPORTANT | Caution –
Making adjustments during distilling

It is sometimes a problem if you reposition a structure during distillation. Remember, the system can become very hot during distillation! You should always have gloves or potholders handy. Then, if necessary, you can intervene during operation without burning your fingers. Due to the different material properties of a hot still, it can be difficult to loosen screwed connections or inserted parts during distilling. With a 0.5-liter model, it is not possible to quickly remove the head from the boiler with a targeted karate chop; the whole still would go flying across the table. We must take a much more cautious approach with legal small-scale stills and hold the boiler firmly in place if we want to loosen the head or any screwed connection prematurely. At the same time, we should always keep one thing in mind: Things are boiling in the boiler! Vapor is rising! Pressure is being created. In the worst case, serious excess pressure can even build up, eventually blowing the head off the boiler. Remember, you do not open a pressure cooker in the middle of cooking. Surely you do not want to burn your hands or face? But do not worry, this sounds worse than it is. I just want you to really know what you are getting into and ensure you take appropriate care.

Is your setup at
the correct
height?

Meanwhile, your still is set up and ready on the table, and you might be wondering what was so hard about doing that. Look at the still closely. Have you considered the height of the installation? Would your system, as it is now constructed, actually be able to distill? Would you be able to collect the distillate from the condenser and easily drain it off it into a suitable container? In the picture on page 49 you can see how here at Destillatio, we distill on special occasions as a team for training purposes. Please take a look at how we have constructed the systems higher up using a wooden board, so we could place the collection container lower down.

Here I have set up the condenser higher up using building blocks.

Setup Height

In fact, very few tabletop stills have a stand of the right height. In almost every case, it is necessary to construct the system higher up—or use a tube to position the run-off appropriately going downward. It is important to make sure that you do not have to rebuild the still while you are operating it. In the picture of the glass still (below), you can immediately see that you almost always have to improvise, unless you have a perfectly equipped laboratory at hand.

Even though the glass flask is elevated on an electric cook top, you have to find some way to be able to set up the collection container correspondingly higher up on the other side of the still. In this case we used a grindstone from the kitchen drawer which by chance was the right height.

At left is the setup of a 0.5-liter column still. Here, the still is placed on a mini electric cook top and the condenser was correspondingly elevated using some building blocks[14] and a glass plate, so that there is room underneath for the glass flask that serves to collect the hydrosol.

A short piece of tube conducts the distillate directly into the flask. In the picture at right you see how I usually solve the height problem in my kitchen. Here an Arabia still is set on the included stand, but I use a suitable tube to conduct the distillate one level lower. There I have set

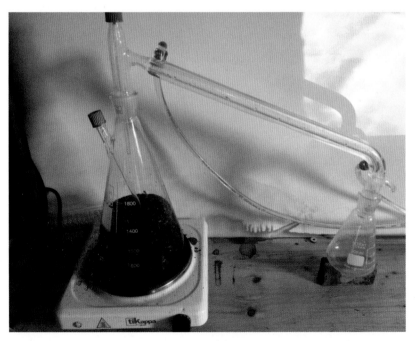

Stabilization using a grindstone that happened to be handy.

---

[14] Here, too, I have improvised. The building blocks did not work very well. The stones got wet because of balancing out the optimum amount of cooling water, and the paint dissolved and left orange color spots everywhere that were difficult to remove.

a board crosswise across the opened kitchen drawer and a measuring glass stands stably and securely on top to collect the distillate.

When setting up your still, you are challenged to think about it and find a suitable solution, depending on your still and your living situation, so you can distill quickly and sensibly. "Raising" the still should become routine.

Condensation

Next to proper construction, we have to think about condensation. Sometimes a well-functioning cooling system is crucial for the overall result, and it is not always easy to place cooling tubes in such a way that the distillate can remain stable and secure. This is one of the reasons why we should seriously consider beforehand which cooling options are available for the upcoming distillation. In the simplest case, just install the system without a cooling circuit. To do this, you can simply insert the hose between the cooling water intake and discharge (see following), or alternatively plug the lower intake with modeling clay, chewing gum, cork, or silicone.

If at this point we are still thinking about how we can cool the distillate if necessary, almost nothing else can go wrong. Normally, with simple distillations, it is enough to fill the condenser with cold water and to refill it between one and three times. If you have an overflow in the condenser this is very easy, and you can then simply pour in cold

The distillate runs smoothly through the tube one level lower.

Here I connected the cooling water discharge to the intake so that nothing runs out.

Here comes the cooling water, thanks to a pump in a bowl of water.

water from a pitcher. The excess hot water flows smoothly, possibly via a tube, into a sink or bucket. Another good possibility is to add ice cubes or, even better, crushed ice. With a little practice, you can simply distill on a table or in the garden without complicated tube and pump constructions.

A real cooling water circuit is the optimal solution!

Even better is a real cooling circuit, which we keep running best with a small water pump. In the picture you see a column still on a counter with a bowl set at a lower level. The cooling water runs out at the top and splashes into the bowl, which is set on a bar stool. Very convenient, but perhaps you wonder why the bowl is set so low? We come here to another problem dealing with small stills, to an area where we have to try things out beforehand and where there is a lot of improvisation. The art is to create a cooling circuit in which the pump supplies enough water to supply the condenser and all the tubes with sufficient cool water. At the same time, the water pumped into the condenser must also drain out again! Often, the water is pumped into the condenser more quickly than it can drain out through the often very thin tube, so we must then slow the pump speed. Many pumps give you the option of regulating water flow, but often this is not enough and the pump delivers even more water at the lowest level than can overflow from the condenser. Then we have to slow it down more by placing the still higher up than the pump. The pump I use can only pump to a height of about twenty-three inches. When I put it on a bar stool below the counter less water runs through it than if it were standing on the counter. These are subtleties you should know about and pay attention to.

Reduce the amount of water = improvise.

Change the height once again?

Test Distillation

The still is now set up securely and you are well prepared for your first distillation. To get to know your system better and try out the individual processes at least once beforehand, I recommend you begin by simply distilling water. To illustrate distillation clearly, in the pictures above I am using a 0.5-liter hennin still, a model that works well for learning and demonstration due to its historical design.

CHECKLIST — Necessary supplies for distilling

To distill, you need a range of items that should always be ready at hand. You may want to set up a distilling box or crate to hold these supplies and tools.

- ☐ Gloves/potholder
- ☐ Mop/cloths
- ☐ Teflon tape for sealing
- ☐ Enough cold water or ice
- ☐ Measuring glass
- ☐ Small bottles
- ☐ Shot glasses
- ☐ Labels/pens for labeling

- ☐ Distilling book for notes
- ☐ Short alcohol meter
- ☐ Pipette
- ☐ Tubes of different diameters
- ☐ Clamp to secure the tubes
- ☐ Fire extinguisher/fire blanket

CHECKLIST — Before starting the distillation

- ☐ Are all parts fastened tightly and securely?
- ☐ Is the height suitable for collecting the distillate?
- ☐ Is the cooling system ready? Run the cooling water circuit for the test or have water and ice cubes ready. Check overflow.
- ☐ Is the electric burner connected or the spirit/gas/gasoline burner filled? Is a lighter ready for lighting?
- ☐ Are there enough collection containers available for the distillate?
- ☐ Do you have sealant ready (silicon tape, clay, rye flour paste)?

- ☐ Can you quickly wipe something up with a cloth if needed?
- ☐ Do you have a potholder or glove handy so you can hold onto something safely?
- ☐ Could you extinguish a fire if necessary (fire blanket/fire extinguisher nearby)?
- ☐ Have you added what you want to distill?
- ☐ Is the kettle full of liquid?
- ☐ Are there measuring instruments ready at hand?
- ☐ Do you have pens or labels nearby to label the distillate?

If you have checked all the points in the checklist you can light the burner and begin distilling.

Hennin still without a condenser—vapor outlet (left) and with condensing using a spray bottle (right).

A still as a room fragrance diffuser and a fragrance lamp?

In the picture (left) you can see how the vapor flows directly out of the swan neck. Unfortunately, you cannot smell it, but here I am using this still as a fragrance lamp with a little vanilla oil and homemade cinnamon hydrosol. Very aromatic, and the scent flows through the room. The boiling point for hydrosols is the same as for water, 212°F. As soon as the water begins to boil, the vapor rises and flows through the swan neck, which you can see very well here. Normally during distilling we would like to collect the vapor once again and keep it, instead of simply letting it stream into the air. The vapor carries the contents that reach us, so we have to think about how we can collect the vapor, and this is best done by condensing. As soon as the vapor reaches a cold surface, its state of aggregation changes from gaseous to liquid. It condenses when it is cold enough, and runs out of the swan neck as a liquid.

Air cooling vs. water cooling?

I just put a bottle over the swan neck (right) and now spray the head and the swan neck with cold water. A rough solution from the past, but you can see how the vapor immediately condenses in the head when it is sprayed with cold water, and instead of vapor, a distillate flows from the swan neck into the bottle. Here, the principle of distillation becomes vividly visible. If you want to learn about temperatures and the interconnections in distillation, then you might also like to run your still without a condenser and experiment. This is interesting in any case, and you will surely come to have the right sense about your still, as well as the processes that take place when you are distilling. If you do everything right and cool your still sufficiently, then you can theoretically recover the essential oil instead of letting it evaporate into the air. Let us return to our water distillation.

In the best case, if your system is set up perfectly, all the seals are sealed one hundred percent, and there is no loss of liquid or vapor, then you can calculate the quantities you can ultimately distill. With 500 ml of water in the boiler, you could theoretically distill 500 ml of water—but only theoretically. A small amount will surely get caught in the still on the way.

Try out your still without a condenser one time!

IMPORTANT	Never distill with an empty kettle

It is also important to make sure that the boiler never becomes completely empty. Otherwise, the copper could overheat, which in turn could lead to material stress and fatigue that in the worst case could even destroy the boiler. Often small accessories such as side handles on the boiler, but also important parts such as the swan neck on the still head, are soldered on. In case of overheating, the solder melts and your still falls apart and becomes unusable. Please ensure that you never distill the kettle until it is empty. If later you are working with mash or herbs in the kettle, the plant material can also get scorched on hard if there is too little water in the boiler. A situation you may know from your kitchen, but it is much easier to clean up a pot with a big opening than in a small 0.5-liter boiler.

Be nice to your still!

When filling full to the brim with 500 ml of liquid, be careful not to distill more than a maximum of 375 ml. Depending on the design of your still, you will usually add less to the kettle to avoid it boiling over. Therefore, when distilling water, plan on losing at least a quarter of it to be sure. If you think your still might be leaking be even more generous. Better to leave too much in the kettle than to destroy the still.

You now light your burners and wait. Depending on how intense your flame is and the actual amount of water in the boiler, it can take up to twenty minutes for the water to boil and for your patience to be rewarded. When you carefully touch the head, you can feel the still slowly heating up and the temperature rising. Then the first droplets come out of the swan neck one by one, until it really starts to drip or even flow.

Have some patience when heating up!

Now the distillation is running and you can familiarize yourself with the temperatures. Feel a few drops of the distillate. Does it feel cool or warm? In the ideal case, it should flow out of the condenser at about 68°F—that is, rather cool. In the hennin still (p. 56) without its own

The distillation is running . . .

condenser, the distillate, at more than 122°F or 140°F, remains too hot to distill essential oils. The optimal temperatures for alcohol are also around 68°F. You should also know that we need a higher temperature to distill water than to distill alcohol, because the boiling point of water is higher than that of a water/alcohol mixture. If you do not want to trust your senses, you can also measure the temperature using a thermometer. To measure the distillate a normal glass thermometer is sufficient; for measuring the cooling water you can conveniently let a floating thermometer float in the condenser. If the temperature is too high, think about how you can lower the temperature more. Adding ice to the cooling water is a great help, but if possible, you can also increase the cooling water flow. Take care that your condenser does not overflow. When distilling water the temperature is not that important, so you can easily ignore cooling to begin with. But you should learn the temperature

Add crushed ice or snow to the condenser!

behavior of your still during this first run and pay attention to what it can do. Regulating its cooling performance is one of the points that becomes important later on, and which you should master in your sleep. Only if you know the limits of your condenser can you intervene if necessary once it gets too hot. Is the temperature of the distillate correct? Then everything seems to be right. Next, carefully put your fingers in the cooling water, but take care: warm water rises to the top. The cooling water can sometimes be quite hot on the surface, even if it still provides enough cooling effect. Here, too, try to develop a sense so that you can recognize the right temperatures and changes as early as possible.

The outside gets fogged up due to the large temperature difference when you add ice to the condenser.

TIP	Several runs

It is best to try out your still at least once without a condenser, a second time with water in the condenser but without a cooling circuit, and a third time with the condenser filled with ice and then with connected cooling water tubes. This way, you will get a good impression of the temperature differences. In the picture at right above you will see an ice-filled condenser. The ice is cold enough to let the humidity in the room condense, which can be seen well on the fogged metal.

Thermometer for Distilling?

Opinions on thermometers vary widely. While many master distillers think a thermometer is the most important and absolutely indispensable component for any distillation, I still believe that a thermometer is unnecessary as long as you trust your own senses. Even in large industrial distilleries individual fractions in the foreshot are ultimately cut by sensation, namely the senses of smell and taste.

The crucial question: Do we distill better with or without a thermometer?

A thermometer can help, but . . .

A thermometer can help you be informed in a timely way, and it is also generally interesting to know the exact temperatures when you are distilling to distill by temperature, but I nevertheless would not recommend it, especially not for mini stills. It is generally said that the temperature of the rising vapor should be measured at the highest point of the still. This starts the dilemma, because what can make sense for meter-high distilleries with many finely adjustable bubble cap trays and intermediate condensing quickly becomes a joke in a 0.5-liter still just a few inches high. There is no measurable temperature difference between the rising vapor, the boiling contents of the kettle, and the swan neck on top! It is also hardly possible to change the temperature range by using a fine tuning process as in industrial fruit schnapps distilleries, or to collect individual fractions due to their vapor temperature. We can only heat the boiler, vaporize the contents, and collect everything that condenses. Here, it does not matter if you distill at 190°F or break off exactly at 197.6°F. This is all "gray" theory, certainly helps to stoke our fears, and takes away from the fun of distilling.

If we were to take into account that all temperature data is valid only under normal weather conditions and at sea level, then we would quickly realize how many errors can be caused by distilling according to the temperature indication, even if you use a very high-quality and perhaps

It will not work like this: homemade setup of flower vase with a thermometer.

even a calibrated thermometer. For example, the Al Ambik® distillation thermometer is an extremely accurate thermometer, which guarantees that temperatures will be accurate to the degree according to German industrial standards. Nevertheless, we keep getting feedback, according to which the thermometer supposedly displays incorrect temperatures, simply because it indicates water often boils not at 212°F, but only at 206.6°F. It is correct like that! Depending on the altitude and weather conditions, the boiling point of water changes—just like that of alcohol. If you live in the mountains, water can boil at considerably lower temperatures. On top of Mount Everest the boiling point is just over 158°F.

Does water really boil at 212°F?

IMPORTANT Trust your senses

But even if the value of a thermometer is often overestimated when distilling, I would not advise you to use one, or even several thermometers. You should not distill just according to the display of your thermometer and try to cut the foreshots or feints on this basis. A thermometer can help to estimate times and temperatures correctly, and in this way it also provides valuable service.

Valuable mixture: the correct sense of the master distiller in combination with a good thermometer.

I use several small glass floating thermometers to check the temperatures of the cooling water, as well as the mash during mashing. These floating thermometers cost only a few dollars and are very easy to clean; they are even dishwasher safe.

In addition, I am currently making friends with a digital laser temperature gun. Even if this way of measuring temperature used to scare me, I am able to obtain very accurate and fast results with it, especially with the mini stills. All you need to do is point the laser at the target while pressing the trigger and the temperature is reliably displayed. Most interesting here above all is the extremely wide temperature range. It is possible to measure the negative temperatures of the ice cubes for the cooling water as well as the high temperatures directly on the burner, or on the cook top. Although most of these temperatures remain unimportant when it comes to distilling, it is a lot of fun to read all sorts of temperatures at all the possible and impossible places. Thanks to the continuous readability you can also get very good results during the distillation and read temperature patterns. Even if we can only measure

Additional thermometers are a support for estimating temperature patterns properly.

the boiler, the head, or the swan neck from the outside, we get good results with a temperature gun. Due to copper's extremely high temperature conductivity, the temperature outside the copper is very similar to the temperature inside, and we can directly induce what is going on in the distillation process. The prices, depending on the quality and manufacturer, range between $23 and $60; I would advise you to purchase such a fine device, especially if your still did not come with a mounted thermometer as standard equipment.

Do mounted thermometers work better?

A high-quality thermometer fastened to the head or swan neck of the still would ultimately be an even better solution, even if it is often impossible to install a proper thermometer here due to the very limited space. I would like to give you a brief overview of the advantages and disadvantages of different types of thermometers for distilling.

> **TIP** | **Use a good thermometer**
>
> And a tip beforehand: if you already distill using a thermometer then please use a good one. If you just want to be able to rely on the results, distilling with a thermometer makes sense!

A Bit of Thermometer Know-How

Glass Thermometer

This is what you should know if you want to work with a glass thermometer!

If you buy a miniature still with a pre-installed thermometer, the probability is very high that it is a glass thermometer. I recommend you take a closer look at your glass thermometer and how it functions, and check the accuracy occasionally. If it has not been stored properly and there are large temperature differences a thermometer can show considerable deviations over time. For years most thermometers have been filled with so-called "self-wetting" liquids, mostly colored red or blue, for environmental protection. In contrast to permanently accurate previously mercury-filled thermometers, these measuring liquids cannot concentrate themselves completely. With each expansion the liquid wets the thermometer walls and a tiny part of the liquid remains "hanging," so to speak, in the tube. In the worst case, the liquid can even dry out and give false results.

> ### TIP Store properly
>
> If possible, store a glass thermometer upright and at as constant a temperature as possible!

Otherwise, most so-called universal thermometers display temperatures quite reliably, even if their readability often leaves something to be desired. There are extra-long glass thermometers available, specially designed for the distillation sector, which can display temperatures in 0.2-degree intervals and therefore remain much more accurate. Furthermore, some thermometers are specifically designed for the higher temperature range during distillation. Most thermometers are adjusted to 68°F and then show the smallest deviations within this temperature range. Special thermometers for distillation can also be set to 140° or 176°F when they are produced.

Universal or special thermometer?

Fortunately, most glass thermometers are easily interchangeable, so if you are interested, you can exchange a potentially too small and difficult-to-read universal thermometer with a more accurate laboratory device. Most mini stills can also be retrofitted by drilling a hole and using a rubber stopper that fits. Glass thermometers usually show ascending temperature changes quickly and reliably, and if there is cooling, are only delayed by a few seconds. If you want to know the temperature exactly, you can also buy a real mercury thermometer from a laboratory supplier. You should be very careful, though, because if the thermometer breaks mercury fumes will be released.

Please take good care with mercury!

Bimetallic Thermometer

Bimetallic thermometers tend to play a subordinate role with legal mini stills, although they have some advantages over glass thermometers. First of all, with bimetallic thermometers it is very easy to "keep tabs" on the temperature due to the intuitively readable measuring scales. Usually a quick glance is enough for you to recognize the temperature. But here you should also note the quality of the thermometer. In the handicrafts area, we often use simple heating thermometers from the hardware store, which I would by no means recommend to you. Heating thermometers react sluggishly to temperature changes and can give you a rough overview of the temperature inside your still.

How accurately can we measure with a thermometer from a hardware store?

Most bimetallic thermometers measure by means of a simple spring made of two metals with different expansion properties under temperature changes. As a result, depending on the temperature on the sensor, the indicator at the end of the spring can be turned and indicate how intense the expansion was on the measuring scale. With this simple method deviations of up to ten percent are not uncommon. Only high-quality industrial thermometers have a fine spiral to ensure an accurate display.

German industrial standards = guaranteed to exact degree.

If you distill using a bimetallic thermometer, then the best thing is to use one that conforms to German industrial standards, because then you can rest assured that your display is guaranteed to be accurate to 1°C. There are specific distilling thermometers commercially available specifically for use in distillation that also display the temperature range important for distilling most accurately and react most quickly.

A disadvantage of bimetallic thermometers is their size; often the relatively large mountings look out of place on a dainty hobby still. If you want to retrofit, it is usually enough to drill a hole and screw in the thermometer, but take care to ensure that the sensor protrudes up to 1.5 inches into the head, and you still have to secure the copper washers and nuts from the inside with screws. Depending on the dimensions of your still this could be quite a tricky matter.

Digital Thermometer

Digital thermometer: What is the modern version good for?

Essentially, I would advise against using a digital thermometer, although the models with fine sensors on long cables would be perfectly suited for measuring the temperature even in the smallest swan neck. Unfortunately, I have not yet discovered a digital thermometer that covers the measuring range we need when distilling. If you read the manufacturers' specifications for digital thermometers, you will surely discover the terms "interval" and "latency." This information is an indication that digital thermometers cannot measure the temperature continuously, but rather deliver a measurement at an interval, such as every two seconds. We can then add the latency time to this, that is, the time required to transport the temperature pulses from the sensor to the digital display via the cable and convert them visibly for us. Unfortunately, the thermometer is therefore no longer fast and would certainly be too slow to really help us when a steam distillation is starting.

Infrared Laser Thermometer

What is great about laser thermometers is the continuous measurement. As long as you are pressing the trigger it displays new measurement results, making it possible to focus on a kettle and watch live as the temperature climbs. You can change the measuring point at any time. It is only important to know that you always measure the surface—that is, the outer surface of the still, not the inside of the kettle. And even if the manufacturer sometimes advertises that you could even measure someone's fever in the next room with such a thermometer, this is not quite correct. The infrared beam radiates out in a funnel shape, meaning the farther away an object is, the more inaccurate and delayed the measurement will be due to the latency time.

Practical: the quick "shot" from the hip.

With all this theoretical knowledge you are now well equipped to finally get to work and do a practical distillation.

Creating Your Own Distillates

I hope the introductions at the beginning of this book did not scare you off too much. With the necessary know-how, you can make great products with a mini still. Distilling is not witchcraft—not even with a small still. We get the fastest and best results as a beginner by making spirits, especially gin! This is a good reason to start this chapter on alcohol with the production of this delicious spirit.

The Spirits That I Summon . . .

Believe me, creating your own spirits with a small still is a true joy. Once you have started, this initially seemingly harmless hobby can quickly become a real addiction, not because of the danger of becoming an alcoholic, but because of the seemingly endless taste nuances that open up for you.

For a spiritualistic invocation, when distilling we conjure up the spirit of alcohol. May the "good" spirit please free the aromas from the alcohol base we use and bring them out to us. The spirit that is later captured in the bottle should continue to reach our palate. If we act appropriately, in a prudent and wise manner, the spirit will be under our spell and will reward our efforts in manifold ways. If we prepare our magic drink properly, and vary or exchange the base smoothly, the newcomer will soon be able to open new, previously uncharted worlds of taste and related "Aha!" experiences. At the same time, actually drawing out the aromas by the spirit of alcohol is not even very difficult or complicated. For your first attempts even a simple still is enough, no matter what the design. It is best at first to try to distill a well-known spirit. You will soon notice how strong the aromas seem to you when you add them and freshly distill out the alcohol. Simply add such typical aroma carriers as juniper, caraway, or anise, together with an alcohol that is as aroma-neutral as possible, into your pot still and heat it up; that is all. After a short time you can taste the first drops of your own juniper, caraway, or anise spirits. Guaranteed fresh and delicious . . .

We call on the spirit of alcohol . . .

Alcohol for Making Spirits

Would you like to make your first attempts easy? Then stay on the safe side with a purchased clear vodka or (double) grain spirits. Both variants have a characteristic neutral taste that you can neutralize more by distilling, but at the same time you can enrich it with the aromas of the "botanicals" you use.

As an alternative, and even more suitable for steeping dry spices or nuts, you can also use a higher proof Primasprit —rectified spirit or neutral spirit in English. Some aromas dissolve better into high-proof

Distilling is not witchcraft!

Primasprit, vodka, or grain spirits = the perfect base alcohol.

alcohol. If you pay attention to the "proof" when shopping, you will soon find an inexpensive, clear rectified spirit in one of the many discount and budget supermarkets around the corner. Or you can use a nearly pure alcohol[15] from the pharmacy. Unfortunately, pharmacy alcohols are very expensive, and it is not necessary to use such a high-proof alcohol for distilling spirits as a hobby. If you indeed want to work with a very high proof alcohol, it is a good idea to macerate the fruit first in a smaller amount of alcohol and then reduce the mixture to about 40% ABV with water before distilling it.

> **IMPORTANT** | **Boiling point**
>
> The higher the alcohol content of your base, the lower the boiling point during distillation, and the more flammable the vapors are.

Or would you prefer wine spirits?

If you are more spiritually inclined, the best way is to use a wine spirit, as recommended by Paracelsus. Either a purchased brandy, or better—because it is neutral in aroma—a high-proof brandy you distilled from a wine. To obtain a clear aroma and higher proof more quickly, you can also buy a brandy and simply distill it again. Rum also works well, but often brings its own flavor into the bouquet. The most inexpensive one to make would be a neutral alcohol distilled from sugar water.

Sample by studying!

Did the aroma that you so easily elicited from your still as a sideline taste good to you? Then you are ready to experiment! Even if you have no other spices other than caraway, anise, and juniper, you could still capture very different flavors. Try it out. It makes a difference whether you distill the "botanicals" directly with a clear vodka, as described, or whether you add the herbs fourteen days beforehand and let them steep. The good spirit of alcohol, the "spirit" of your spirits, will provide your taste buds with different aromas, depending on the process used.

---

[15] As a rule, you cannot distill an alcohol to more than 95% ABV. If you buy chemically produced higher-proof alcohols at the pharmacy they will be reduced to 95% ABV just due to humidity.

If you let the herbs steep longer the aromas become more intense, and often also fuller and rounder—but only sometimes. At the same time, some aromas which are not so volatile and secondary materials are released. The distillate can develop additional tart, perhaps even bitter, aromas. Ultimately, it is your own sense of taste that decides whether this will be an advantage or a disadvantage. Often bitter tones are desired and just round off a flavor experience. Let your tongue decide and create your own preferences.

Trust your own preferences!

TIP — Trying out something new

Strictly speaking, it does not matter which base you use for hobby distilling. Even a strongly aromatic fruit wine would contribute to a unique taste experience after distillation if the aromas from the original drink preserve themselves in the spirit and harmonize with the added herbs, fruits, and spices. You may and you should experiment and have fun, as well as collect experiences and tastings. And remember, in a hobby everything is permitted, as long as the size of the still does not exceed legal provisions.

Important: You can also have fun while distilling!

IMPORTANT — Making spirits according to law

Regulation (EC) No 110/2008 of the European Parliament clearly defines the legal requirements for what constitutes types of *Geist* ("spirit"— There are traditional differentiations among types of such distilled spirits in German-speaking countries, such as between *Geist* and *Spirituosen* [liquors]).

... and what does the law say?

1. A *Geist* may only be made from low-sugar fruits or berries. Sugar-containing fruits such as pears, apricots, cherries, etc., may not be used and should be mashed and processed into a fine brandy.
2. Nothing other than alcohol and a flavor carrier may be added. For example, hazelnuts and rectified spirit produce a hazelnut *Geist*. Adding other nuts would not be permitted!
3. Distillates that are flavored by macerating different spices, but also flowers or vegetables, etc., which are subsequently distilled off, are by law not *Geist*, but *Spirituosen* (liquors).

You can see that EU regulations also intervene strongly in making *Geist,* which is probably also good for us consumers. This way, we can be sure that we are buying a real *Haselnussgeist* (hazelnut spirits) or *Himbeergeist* (raspberry brandy) when we visit an unknown distillery. The laws prevent anyone from misleading us with artificially flavored industrial alcohol and offering it as a "true *Geist.*" Artificially flavored drinks must also be labeled as liquors or liqueurs.

As hobby distillers, we do not have to comply with commercial regulations.

Fortunately, as hobby distillers we do not have to stick to this. As hobby distillers, we do not have to comply with the legal regulations. In home distilling, we can mix ingredients by preference, or make a pear or flower *Geist.* Privately, we can even go a few steps farther and distill "unthinkable" spirits. Whatever you like is allowed! Theoretically, you can distill everything. For example, distill the rest of the gingerbread from the Christmas baked goods with mulled wine for a very "Christmasy" spirit. Or a few pieces of Serrano ham in brandy in honor of Andalusia. Let your imagination run wild and enjoy these freedoms you would never be able to enjoy as a commercial distiller. It is not all that bad; in some applications we hobby distillers even have the advantage.

Of course, we can also name and label our brandies and spirits as we please. We cannot sell them, but can certainly give them as presents!

Steam Distillation

Have you been experimenting with and gotten to know your still? For example, with different soaking or macerating times? Could you notice differences in flavor? Here the still becomes a steam machine. You will certainly be happy about the potential to distill out the finest aromas from your plant materials using steam distillation.

Here we distill with a steam engine!

Here, you put the flavor carriers in a separate vapor chamber set above the still's boiler, and they are then perfused through the alcoholic spirits after heating. The spirit comes into contact with the plant material only briefly and will capture and carry only the finest and particularly light volatile aromas and essential oils. A refined process that leads to particularly fine nuances, depending on the type of plant used, but it sometimes also produces less aromatic results than if the plants, spices, or herbs are added directly to the kettle. As a general rule, you can distill all plants that contain essential oils by steam especially well and always achieve aromatic results. But just as you can still make herbal distillates (hydrosols) from plants that do not contain much oil, we can also make aromatic alcohols from many plants, such as raspberries, oranges, or pears, or at least strengthen the aroma.

As you can see, you can decisively influence the result just by the type of distillation. What do you think about how much the result changes when you vary the amount of the plants or mix different plants together? The best thing is to just try it out. The following are some more practical hints about my favorite drinks.

Distilling Spirits with a Small Still

Anise

Anise is often underestimated, or not seen as an ingredient for "normal" drinks. Anise has so many flavors, and at the same time is easy to work with. For this reason alone we should work with anise more. When an "Ouzo" is put on the table in a Greek restaurant, it becomes clear it has hidden depths of something very aromatic. From Turkey we know "Raki," which becomes "Arak" in its more Arabic neighbors. In Spain you get an "Anis" in sweet or dry; mixed with brandy it becomes "Sol y Sombra" (sun and shade). In France, "Pastis" is poured together with water because of its beautiful milky cloudiness, and in Italy "Sambuca" is served with a coffee bean. All these drinks have one thing in common: they are distillates with anise. If we look more closely, we also find anise as an ingredient in absinthe, gin, and in different herbal schnapps. The production processes and the possibilities for using it are as varied as the many varieties of anise schnapps. For Ouzo, anise can be added with the mash and fermented together with the other ingredients, or simply macerated in any favorite alcohol. As a third version, anise also works extremely well for immediate distillation and can be distilled by steam and directly in the boiler. But this is by no means all, because anise can be initially distilled off with water as an essential oil and later re-added to the alcohol—a process often used in making liqueurs. Anise flavors are also popular in the industry, which is why you can buy such a wide range of different types of premixes and flavorings to make beverages.

Anise is so easy to distill and at the same time so versatile . . .

Anis, Sambuca, Ouzo, Raki, Pastis . . .

"Only a fool makes
no experiments."
–Charles Darwin

TIP Experiment

For a pure anise flavor experience, I recommend you distill half a bottle of white wine in your still's boiler with three tablespoons of anise seeds (about forty grams). Since the wine usually contains only about 10% alcohol by volume you can taste the result directly after distilling it, with about 40% ABV the total result. With about 375 ml of wine, you should be able to distill a sufficient quantity to fill two or three 20 ml schnapps glasses. Let yourself savor the taste —this is an Anis in its purest form.

It would also be interesting to put a sample in a test tube and make another attempt. Put the same amount of anise in a canning jar or bottle with the other half of the wine bottle and let it steep for a week before distilling. Compare the results.

Third, try the same thing again by distilling the anise with vodka or grain spirits. Here, the result will come out at a significantly higher proof and you should dilute it with distilled or filtered water until you reach a drinking strength of about 40% ABV. Compare it again . . .

Here we are distilling anise with vodka in a two-liter pot still.

Many anise spirits have added flavor carriers. This is officially permitted, as long as anise remains the main ingredient and the drink later also tastes of anise. In hobby distilling, you can mix in whatever you like. Experiment further by adding small amounts of fennel, caraway, or licorice.

Gin and Genever

Do you like gin? Then I can guarantee you a lot of fun with a tabletop still. It is difficult to achieve such quick, uncomplicated, and delicious results with any other type of alcohol. The possible variations are endless, and there is plenty of room for your own creations.

My tip: Familiarize yourself with the possibilities of gin distillation!

But the best thing about gin is the quantity we can obtain with a small still. If we try to fiddle something with purchased *Doppelkorn* (at least 38% ABV grain spirits) and we understand ourselves not as a master stillman but as a distiller, we can easily produce ten liters of the finest gin in one run. I will tell you about gin at the end of this section. With gin, anything is allowed, and there are many ways to make it.

We can produce ten liters of gin with a mini still!

Originally gin was a simple, brutally rough grain liquor made palatable only by the addition of juniper. In the sixteenth century, freshly distilled grain liquor was relatively cheap to produce, but in the early years of the craft of distilling it was not for everyone. Resourceful master distillers came to the idea of flavoring the fiery grain flavor of their liquors with the strong aroma of juniper, which was cultivated everywhere in our latitudes. Each master distiller found his own recipe and mixed in other spices, fruits, or herbs (botanicals).

Herbs and spices for the distiller.

Despite the colorful spices, gin is colorless as it drips from the still.

Uniquely versatile thanks to more than 120 botanicals!

Today, we know of up to 120 different ingredients for often secret gin recipes. There is really plenty of leeway for you here, and you will probably not be able to try out and taste all the facets and blends that are possible with gin in just one lifetime. For this reason master distillers often experiment with small tabletop stills in their search for new flavor experiences. Distillers distill individual flavors in small stills and then mix these later with a neutral grain liquor to create a round, harmonious flavor experience. Just like in the hobby area, masters are able to discover completely new aroma notes in an uncomplicated way, or try out special compositions. And what the master distillers can do with such a miniature still you have already been able to do at home for a long time! Try it out; you can find most of the basic ingredients in your kitchen cabinets.

TIP Basic recipe

To 500 ml of neutral grain spirits, first add up to a maximum of 20 g (four tablespoons) of juniper berries. I recommend chopping the berries, which goes very quickly with an immersion blender with a chopper attachment. Then 10 g is often enough, since juniper is relatively intense in taste. If you want distilling to develop into a hobby, I would recommend you purchase a good food processor and chopper. It will be worth it to chop plant material before adding it, and you will save yourself a lot of work if you do not have to work with a knife or a mortar.

The maceration for making gin: grain spirits with spices.

TIP Recipe variation

In the original Dutch genever (Dutch gin), the botanicals were added during mashing, contributing to a "more hearty" flavor, but you can barely taste the subtleties of the different spices. If you want to go this route use a grain mash, and after lautering the grain, cook it with the appropriate flavor carriers. Proceed as if you were adding the hops to a beer. This gives you a good and easy-to-use spicy base for your own genever. I would like to recommend the twenty-liter model Braumeister® (Brewmaster) by Speidel for making grain mash. With this appliance, you can program the individual steps up to lautering, and then you can program in cooking the spices and save yourself a lot of work (more on this later).

The juniper berries are only the main ingredient. Depending on the type, other flavor carriers are added. Trust your own preferences and add more "botanicals" to taste to the maceration. When starting out, your own gins, which are distilled from "only" three or four more ingredients, work better. Also, it may make sense to add the juniper separately from the rest or let it steep for a few days longer.

A gin must taste like juniper!

Only when you are more secure about the harmony of the composition should you try using several ingredients at the same time and distill more delicacies.

Fennel, anise, pimento, coriander, cardamom, peppercorns, cinnamon, and ginger work especially well as "botanicals," but so do herbs, such as rosemary, laurel or lavender, and lemon, grapefruit, or orange peel. When using citrus fruits, it is advisable to remove the white part of the peel to avoid bitter sub-aromas.

The most delicious ingredients from the spice rack.

For our much finer genuine gin, we macerate the botanicals with a neutral alcohol from the pharmacy, a rectified spirit, or with a clear *Doppelkorn*. At this point, we can once again decide whether to allow the ingredients to steep for up to fourteen days, whether we will distill immediately, or whether we distill out the alcohol using steam. Let yourself be surprised by the differences. According to the quantities from the outset you must have macerated just under 600 ml, and you can now easily divide this mixture into two parts, distill them off in a mini still, and compare the differences. It would be even better if you prepare an entire liter at the same time, and thus have enough starting material of the same quality and composition so you can try out all three version and compare them to each other. And when you really compare

Macerated grain spirits with turmeric and other spices before and after distillation.

the macerations to each other, then I advise you to use a fourth method! Macerate your botanicals in the alcohol and just filter them out. This is no longer a *Geist*, but more like an alcohol maceration, which you can also see from the color. Gin is usually colorless, because the color of the macerated herbs is not passed along through distillation. Depending on the ingredients, an alcohol maceration can be very intensely colored (see the yellow maceration in the previous picture due to the fresh turmeric root). Only the "purification" of the alcohol in a still changes the intense yellow maceration into a clear, aromatic distillate. In the United States, you can get "do-it-yourself gin packages" which contain a bottle of grain spirits and some herbs. These should be mixed and filtered. An interesting maceration, but not real gin! Simply try out all the different methods, and perhaps you will discover the next "lifestyle" gin or a unique new aroma combination that will become internationally established. At the moment, gin distilleries with unique, new aromas are coming out of the woodwork—and many of them are experimenting with small tabletop stills just as we are.

The agony of choice? A wide selection at Stefan Bierbaum's gin seminars (www.der-destillateur.de).

| TIP | For anyone in a hurry! |

With the small quantities that we hobby distillers work with, it is not always fun to let your maceration just stand. It works more quickly when we put all the ingredients into a food processor or a smoothie maker and mix them well, or puree them with an immersion blender. This lets you swirl intense aromas into the alcohol within minutes and then distill them off again shortly afterward. Please use organic citrus fruits so that you do not distill the contaminants that remain on the peel of conventional products.

| TIP | Without distilling |

Mix essential oils—with the juniper oil leading the way—drop-by-drop into a clear grain spirit. Essential oils combine inextricably with the alcohol and help create an intense aroma. Be sure to use genuine and natural essential oils, and if possible naturally organic quality.

An uncomplicated gin to mix yourself—if necessary, without having to distill it yourself.

Create a gigantic
variety of different
flavor concentrates!

TIP   For those who savor

If you are serious about savoring different flavors and want to create your own fine gins as a connoisseur then we know another way to obtain delicious gins. Distill each ingredient individually with the same amount of alcohol. You get clearly different flavored alcohols which you can blend together with a pipette and savor. This way, you slowly touch on the perfect flavor. If you carefully measure the quantities at the same time and record the results, later, when you have found your perfect personal gin, you can reproduce the same flavor in greater style, or a year later again distill and blend the same gin.

TIP   Professional tip for a large quantity . . .

The secret of the
distiller—distill
essences and taste
them with grain
spirits.

. . .or how we can produce ten liters of the finest gin with a mini still

As in the previous tip for the savorers, first distill the juniper in a very intense concentration. To do this, add 200 ml of crushed juniper berries to 200 ml *Doppelkorn*, let it all steep for ten days, and then distill out a highly concentrated juniper essence.

In the second step, mix about 30 ml of your favorite flavor carriers together. Also here you will often get more flavor a bit later. To start, you should leave it at three, or a maximum of five different botanicals. Add these with 250 ml *Doppelkorn* to your still and distill a flavor essence from it.

It is really interesting to occasionally taste the brew during the distillation. It is best to prepare several small collecting jugs and distill into different fractions to be able to enjoy the aromatic subtleties during the distillation process. It is indeed impressive how extremely different the taste of a distillate from the same herbal mixture can be depending on whether you tasted it at the beginning, in the middle, or near the end of the distillation. An experience you should not miss out on! According to your personal taste, you can then decide to combine the individual fractions or use only individual portions of them. This is how you finally preserve the aroma concentration in your gin.

Savor to
perfection . . .

In the third step, as the "blend master," you are allowed to savor to your full satisfaction. Fill a container with 100 ml of *Doppelkorn* and use a pipette to carefully add 0.5 to 2 ml of juniper essence, according to taste. For a fine gin with light note of juniper 0.5 ml is often enough.

If you want a stronger juniper tone, for example, to enjoy the gin later with tonic water as a gin and tonic, you may add up to 1.5 ml or a maximum of 2 ml of the previously distilled juniper essence.

Next, carefully mix in—best drop-by-drop—the flavor essence you distilled in the second step. Depending on the desired intensity of the notes of herbs, just a few drops can be sufficient to create a truly delicious and harmonious gin—but it can also be one hundred drops, or several milliliters. It is important to write down the ratio in which you stirred each essence into the 100 ml. Only this way can you calculate the required quantities for five or ten liters.

Mix in the flavors with the pipette, drop-by-drop . . .

Normally, you should have distilled enough juniper and flavor essence to be able to easily mix up to ten liters. Try it out; you will be surprised at the professional results you can come up with using such simple methods and so little effort. Combine this method with the previously described method of savoring, and you will soon have a handsome collection of pre-distilled intense flavor essences and can make gin tasting an integral part of your hobby as a distiller. In no other area is it as easy to legally obtain such large quantities and qualities as when making gin. By the way, the industry works using the same methods and tricks to always ensure a consistent quality.

Your results: Ten liters of the finest gin!

Not only do you see the incredible variety of possible botanicals, but also the widely different methods of production; a diversity that is there to discover in gin making. Just get started; you will surely get a lot of fun out of it. By law, gin is a liquor, not a *Geist*! It is hard to do anything wrong, even if you professionally produce and fill your personal recipe later on and have it bottled, or even go into gin making once you discover your recipe.

Gin training with master distiller Stefan Bierbaum (www.der-destillateur.de).

Himbeergeist (Raspberry Brandy)

In making *Himbeergeist*, you can also improvise as with all other spirits and try out all sorts of different production methods. What you enjoy is allowed; what tastes good is allowed. My own home specialty is a *Himbeergeist* which, according to law, is no longer a *Geist*, because I offer it not as clear liquor, but in an appealing rosé and use a few little tricks to increase the amount. Thus, with two or three distillations I comfortably get several bottles full and can enjoy it for the entire year. The recipe was created spontaneously, because I did not want to throw away a lot of raspberry leftovers.

Himbeergeist— or how I doctor up a fine spirit for more yield.

It all started with my wife's raspberry jam—the best jam in the world. Because our little ones do not like any seeds in their jam, my wife first sieves the raspberries through a "Flotte Lotte" food mill. This leaves so many appetizing leftovers that I repented and wanted to make use of them. I quickly decided to macerate the fruity raspberry puree and some fresh raspberries in vodka and let it all steep overnight. (Always pour alcohol over the fresh (or frozen) raspberries and do not let it steep for more than two or three days, because otherwise the flavor of the rather bitter seeds may come through.) I passed the maceration through a sieve and initially got a maceration with an intense raspberry fragrance, which you could have already drunk as it was. But I wanted to distill it.

Very simple: Macerate raspberries in vodka or grain spirits and distill.

I put most of the macerated vodka and raspberry mixture into the boiler of my beloved Arabia still and distilled a delicious real *Himbeergeist* while adding some fresh raspberries to the kettle and the infusion basket. Here you have to be careful not to fill the kettle too much, because otherwise the colored raspberry mixture could boil over and the spirit would get mixed up with the leavings in the boiler. This would not be a problem as long as it tastes good. It is more aromatic if you carefully cut the very high-proof *Himbeergeist* after distilling it with filtered or distilled water to a drinking strength of 40% ABV.

Pour vodka over the raspberries.

Press out the liquid again.

Add a few raspberries to the boiler and distill.

Mix with water (or juice) to drinking strength.

Since you are using a purchased vodka, which has already been purified of foreshots and feints, as your base, you can distill without any concern and collect the distillate starting with the first drop. At the same time this is a very high proof distillation, since the original base with the vodka/raspberry mixture still contains 25% to 35% ABV. You can easily obtain more than 250 ml of *Himbeergeist* in drinking strength per distillation. In three runs you can easily fill a large liquor bottle.

Here you can also save cutting the foreshots and feints . . .

TIP | **Sweetening spirits**

You also drink with your eyes. If you want to surprise a lady who tends to drink something weak with a homemade gift, it may be necessary to cut the distillate with raspberry juice and some sugar instead of water, possibly down to 30% ABV. Thus it is no longer a *Geist* by law, but despite this, a fine gift in the form of a high-proof and very fruity raspberry liqueur. Alternatively, you can also mix it with the maceration. I like to do this, because this way I quickly get a larger quantity, even if it is only described as a liquor, or *Spirituose*.

With or without sugar?

Brandy

You have now been able to gain several good experiences distilling spirits, and know how your still works and how you can make a purchased neutral alcohol aromatic and change its taste. But we have other ways to transform and improve bought finished alcohol. We can transform a wine into a brandy by distillation. This is really very simple and works with any still. Try it out!

Depending on the alcohol content the results will vary. Traditionally, brandies are distilled from young and acidic white wines with rather low alcohol content (and price). This is logical, because why should anyone distill a good drinkable or even high-quality wine? Ultimately, it makes little difference for hobby distillers which wine you use—everything is allowed, as long as it is fun and tastes good. Nevertheless, it would be a shame to turn a good wine into aroma-neutral alcohol. Wines that should be aged for a long time may be highly sulfuric, to prolong their durability. The sulfur aroma thus produced can become unpleasantly

Delicious brandy from an acidic white wine?

conspicuous during distillation and remain in the distillate. You can shake fresh brandy vigorously and aerate it with oxygen before you taste it; this eliminates the pungent vapors to a large extent and the initially unpleasant aroma becomes much milder. Copper can also bind sulfuric acid and will contribute as a catalyst to a harmonious taste experience. Despite these two possibilities, it is more advantageous to get rid of the sulfur from the very beginning. In the industry, sodium silicate water is added before distillation to bind with the sulfur, but I would not recommend this method. It is better to increase the amount of copper that comes into contact with the alcohol vapor by filling the vapor chamber of your still with copper wool and furbishing the head before distilling. But do not worry, this sounds worse than it is.

Always distill wine in copper to remove the sulfurous aromas!

I recommend you keep some bottles of an inexpensive organic white wine in reserve. You might be lucky and even find a type that is made without sulfur. Then you always have a good base for making your own brandy that you can later use in liqueurs or for other recipes with a good conscience. In addition, you can distill away your opened bottles, especially if the wine did not taste good. Thus, you will gradually learn the differences in the aroma that are also due to grape varieties and ingredients.

Invest in a selection of inexpensive organic white wine to distill . . .

Depending on the type of wine, the alcohol content can vary between 8% and 14% ABV. Stronger liqueurs, fortified wines, and port wines are already fortified with brandy to a higher alcohol content. With natural fermentation, it is only possible to obtain a maximum 16% ABV, since normal yeasts die off in higher alcohol concentrations. Nevertheless, we can distill "fortified" wines very well. The higher the alcohol content, the higher the yield will be. In brandy, the aroma comes from the aging, rather than from the grape variety of the distilled wine.

In the industry brandy is always distilled twice, with the resulting heart at the end of the fine spirit distillation being at least 56% ABV, so it is of the necessary purity and quality. According to the law, brandy can even be distilled up to 94% ABV. This is a clear indication that the grape variety and the original flavor are not really important in some brandies, as the aroma actually does not matter. At this alcohol concentration, there is no longer any "place" for the aroma, which only emerges in such a distillation through long aging in an oak barrel and subsequent cutting to drinking strength.

NOTE   Alcohol content

Just by calculation, we can expect a maximum of 100 ml of pure alcohol per liter from a 10% ABV wine. Please note that it is impossible to actually obtain pure alcohol. Even with the best stills, it is impossible to obtain more than a maximum of 97.4% ABV! It is mathematically theoretical if we take 100% ABV as the basis of calculation. As a rule, we will distill out much less alcohol! To get a feel for the possible yield, it is nevertheless good to keep the maximum achievable quantity in mind. Then you do not need to expect any more and can end the distillation in good time.

There is no pure alcohol!

Realistically, we can also fill little more than 400 ml into our legal German 0.5-liter tabletop still. This is an amount that would contain just under 40 ml of pure alcohol. The calculated amount will also be lower due to losses during distillation and the alcohol residues in the boiler. To compensate some for these losses we can dilute the distillate again at the end to a drinking strength of about 40% ABV.

I make it simple for myself and double the 40 ml pure alcohol we calculate that our wine contains to 80 ml, because I do not want to obtain the distillate later in 100% purity, but would like it at drinking strength. Theoretically calculated, the 80 ml would be an alcohol of 50% ABV! Due to the losses described above I have to round it off further. The 80 ml in 50% ABV strength would still be impossible, by calculation and in theory! I keep the 80 ml as an amount, but go down further in the percentage to a drinking strength of 38% ABV. This would be a scenario in which, by distilling 400 ml of a 10% ABV wine, I could finally distill 80 ml of brandy of drinking strength. With this simple calculating trick you get an idea of what might be possible before distilling if everything works perfectly. As a rule, your yield will come out slightly lower, because you have to cut the foreshots and have to interrupt the distillation before all the alcohol is distilled out of the wine. Nevertheless, with ten distillations, you can ultimately fill a 0.75-liter liquor bottle. It is better if you get used to smaller liquor bottles when distilling brandy. Commercially available 200 ml bottles are a good size for hobby distilling.

The truth: You get only 80 ml of brandy per any legal 500 ml distillation.

You need a weekend to fill a 0.75-liter bottle with home-distilled brandy!

The alcohol meter renders useful service during distilling.

Simple Brandy Distilling

In a hobby everything is allowed, as long as it brings happiness. Therefore, I would first like to describe the "fun version," in which you can distill a small amount of fresh brandy without much effort. The fun version is ideal for demonstrations or social gatherings, if you want to see what you will get out of a distillation, or if you simply want to distill away the remains in a wine bottle. This type of distilling is the only intended use for many of the small party and fun stills.

And that is how it works: Add the wine to be distilled as a base to the boiler of your still. Take care not to overfill the kettle so that nothing will bubble up through the swan neck when the wine is boiling. You should fill the still to three-quarters at most, then heat it slowly and wait until the system becomes warm and the first droplets of your distillation fall gently out of the condenser.

IMPORTANT	Cut the foreshots

Please remember to collect the first drops separately and not consume them! Even when distilling purchased wine the foreshots should be cut! You can assume that the amount of the foreshots is very low. Some stills are specially equipped with a small collecting cup for this purpose. If you capture about a thimbleful at the beginning and do not mix it with your drinking alcohol—the immediately following heart or middle cut—then you are on the safe side. In most cases, the foreshots will come out in a significantly smaller amount. For hobby distilling, the following applies: If you are not sure, cut too much rather than too little!

Remove harmful substances!

Whatever flows from your still after this first thimbleful you can taste with a clear conscience. Meanwhile, hold your finger (or a small spoon) under the fresh, dripping distillate and taste it drop-by-drop—or better, have several small containers ready and distill in many different small fractions. This allows you to monitor the progress of the flavor very well, as well as the decreasing alcohol content over the entire distillation, and you can also decide later which fraction belongs to the delicious heart and which one you would rather not use.

We only distill what tastes good!

If the distillate only tastes flat and dull then end the distillation. Theoretically, in such a distillation, you should get a sufficient amount to be able to easily fill two to three shot glasses.

Note that when distilling alcohol, the first drops—starting with the foreshots—can be extremely high proof. Since the alcohol content of the vapor decreases during the course of the distillation, the temperature in the boiler increases at the same time. The distillate becomes more watery in the course of the distillation. A wine, like all other alcohol bases, should be regarded as a water/alcohol mixture. The boiling point of alcohol, at about 172°F, is well below that of water, which starts to boil at 212°F.[16] Because of these different boiling points, it is only possible to distill the alcohol out of the water. Alcohol evaporates at significantly lower temperatures, and therefore rises through the swan neck long before the water does. Nevertheless, even the finished distillate always remains an alcohol/water mixture! It is not possible to heat the boiler to "only" 172°F and distill the alcohol out first; the transition between the two boiling points fluctuates. The higher the temperature, the more water you will also distill, and the lower the proof of the distillate will be. In practice, you will be able to start distilling at a temperature of 180°F at the earliest and end the distillation at 198°F, even if there is still residual alcohol in the boiler. At the end of the distillation, the vapor mixes more and more with the heavier fusel oils and portions of the feints, which would harm the aroma of our brandy, so we break the distillation off at an early stage to not dilute the "fine" heart or damage its taste. In all, the total result of your first distillation will now be about 40% ABV and can be tasted directly or further processed. Cheers . . .

We distill from the very high proof to the watery.

Important to know: The transition is always fluid!

---

[16] At least at normal atmospheric pressure and at sea level.

Dealing with Contaminants in Distilling

Can you be blinded by homemade alcohol?

Since we have learned a lot about distilling and can create spirits as well as our own brandy, and have tasted the first drops and are ready to go on, it is now time to deal seriously with contaminants. In fact, you can do some things wrong when distilling alcohol. Everyone knows the rumors that you can fatally poison yourself or the high likelihood that you can be blinded after trying home-distilled schnapps. For example, I now need glasses because I suffer from presbyopia. Not to worry, my eyesight has not gotten worse due to distilling schnapps.[17] My eye doctor thinks that it is completely normal and it is simply age-related far-sightedness. Nevertheless, we must not underestimate the dangers and should simply toss away the first droplets or keep them separate during each alcoholic distillation. There remain great differences in the amount of expected flow depending on what we cleanly mash and distill. With a bit of expert knowledge and logical thinking, we can very quickly become very safe and give away or enjoy our home-distilled drinks with a clear conscience.

"Clean" mash = few contaminants.

First, we must distinguish among an already distilled alcohol, a beer, a wine, a fruit mash, or a grain mash. If we know what we are distilling and how "cleanly" the product was originally made then we can better estimate the "danger." A purchased 96% ABV rectified spirit from the pharmacy will contain barely any contaminants; here we get a product of the highest possible purity, which can save us from having to cut the foreshots later on. It is simply important to know and understand the differences. If you use a purchased brandy, grain spirit, or vodka, the result may appear different. Generally, you can assume that for these, the foreshots were already cut professionally and you hardly have to reckon with any contaminants. But you should also know that the transition from the foreshots to the heart is just as fluid as the transition from alcohol to water in our previous explanations about brandy. In fact, it is not possible to distill an alcohol completely without a portion of foreshots. The master distiller[18] decides on the moment to cut the main portion of the foreshots and when he would like to start with the fine heart.

---

[17] You do not get impaired vision from alcohol by distilling schnapps, but from drinking schnapps.

[18] In industrial distilleries, the individual fractions are often only cut based on certain different temperatures.

Master distiller Michael Weber engaged in making a sensory cut of the foreshots.

In every "normal" drinking alcohol, especially fruit schnapps and brandies, portions of the foreshots are retained. If we use a purchased, already purified alcohol, we can thus cut a little of the foreshots anyway and improve our alcohol even more. These are only a few single drops. As hobby distillers, we can gladly accept this small loss from the total yield for the sake of safety and a better aroma.

It is also interesting to know that foreshots contaminants are present in much smaller quantities in grain mashes than if you are distilling fruit brandies. A difference we should know about! With this knowledge, it becomes clear why we should expect fewer contaminants in a grain spirit or vodka than in a fruit brandy. And it becomes clear why it is better that we use a neutrally distilled grain spirit or vodka for making a *Geist* in a mini still. These usually contain the least amount of contaminants, and as beginners, it is hard for us to do anything wrong. Apart from the fact that grain spirits usually contain fewer contaminants, a grain spirit or vodka is often deliberately made in a high proof, sometimes to over 80% ABV. This achieves a higher purity in the alcohol than in the case for wine or fruit brandies, which may still contain aromas, and for this reason, depending upon the type, are distilled to what is definitely a low proof.

Every distilled drink still contains portions of foreshots!

Grain liquors are often "purer" than fruit brandies.

Distilling in a mini still = no risks.

I do not want to stop you from distilling. Strictly speaking, mini stills in the legal 0.5-liter size are so small that potential amounts of possible contaminants are extremely small and could hardly affect you. Nevertheless, I recommend that you pour out the first droplets from each distillation to be safe. With purchased high-proof alcohols, this really amounts to just a few drops. With wine or beer, small amounts—perhaps a thimbleful—are likewise enough if you want to be safe. You should really take care, and if necessary, cut a little more if you are processing your own fruit mashes. Here, as long as you are impeccably hygienic when making your mash and the fermentation proceeds without problems, it will only contain small quantities of contaminants. In case of doubt, simply cut somewhat more and you can be certain. If you are uncertain, you can also have several tiny collection containers (i.e., test tubes) at hand and distill single portions, perhaps 10 ml per glass, in several different fractions. This gives you the opportunity to subsequently evaluate the distilled out portions individually as "good" or "bad" with your sense of smell, and either pour them away—or add them to the heart.

What Are the Foreshots?

Methanol has a low boiling point of just 149°F, and will evaporate before the actual drinking alcohol (ethanol) during the alcohol distillation and get to the condenser through the still. Methanol collected in larger amounts is used as a cleaning agent and solvent, or as a fuel for internal combustion engines. Methanol is not very toxic at first and can easily be excreted by the kidneys or lungs in smaller amounts up to 0.1 g per kilogram of body weight. In case of serious poisoning, the effects of intoxication occur, as with alcohol, followed by headaches, nausea, weakness, and vomiting as a result of a disturbance of the body's acid/base balance. In the course of this disturbance, the nerves, especially the optic nerve, can be attacked and at times irreparably damaged. For fruit brandies, the permitted methanol content is limited to fifteen grams per liter. What is interesting is that at first, the decomposition product of methanol in the body is responsible for the symptoms of poisoning, and you can prevent them, or at least slow them down, by drinking ethanol.

If you inadvertently drink a larger amount of methanol, it is advisable to consume a good drinking alcohol until you can get medical treatment. This prevents degradation of the methanol and can thus prevent damage to the nerves.

> Methanol can largely be avoided due to its low boiling point.

Ethyl acetate is another substance that we often find in the foreshots, because it reaches its boiling point at 170.6°F, and therefore drips out of the swan neck shortly before our actual heart. Fortunately, the liquid called ethyl acetate (or acetic acid ethyl ester) and the distinctive "glue odor," which many consider "delicious," can be recognized relatively readily.

Ethyl acetate is used as a strong solvent in nail polish remover or to extract caffeine, but also as a flavoring agent in all kinds of artificial ingredients for confectionery products. It is the "intoxicating" substance in glue that so-called glue sniffers like to sniff and can damage brain cells. On the skin, ethyl acetate is a strong degreasing agent and can cause irritation, so you should not be tempted to use the foreshots for cosmetics. Here again, the heart—our ethanol—is the healthier version.

> Ethyl acetate can be recognized by its scent . . .

What Is the Heart?

Ethyl alcohol is the substance we are seeking . . .

Ethyl alcohol is the drinking alcohol for which we have been waiting. As already described, the boiling point of drinking alcohol is about 172.4°F, and it emerges somewhat later than the ethyl acetate. The transition is fluid, and the actual art of distilling is to be able to change over from the foreshots to the heart as early as possible, and as late as necessary. Not only to keep losses low, but also because with fruit schnapps, the most aromatic and therefore the finest alcohols change over directly to the distillate right at the beginning. For most other liquors the difference is not that big, and you might like to cut somewhat later for safety's sake. The higher proof alcohol we distill, the higher the purifying effect and the more neutral the aroma that will come out. For hobby distilling, we are usually not interested in a pure ethyl alcohol, but want fine and intense aromas. For this reason, we always carefully cut the first drops at the start to the best of our knowledge and conscience, but also accept the truth that the foreshots and the feints contribute to the individually different characteristic aromas of our liquors, and that we have little to fear in terms of health.

What Are the Feints?

In the end, it is all just booze . . .

In distilling, the feints (or tails) consist of a collection of various ingredients—for example, various fusel oils and acids—that all have something in common: their boiling point is clearly higher than that of our drinking alcohol. The closest to our distillation temperatures is propanol, with a boiling point of 206.6°F. Propanol smells like drinking alcohol and causes intoxication symptoms, dizziness, and numbness.

Mini alembic still in the kitchen.

Propanol can also severely irritate the skin. Since our distillations usually become watered down at 197.6°F and taste soapy, in most cases we break the distillation off well before the boiling point of propanol, and it is highly unlikely that propanol will end up in our liquor in any dangerous quantity.

Also contained in the feints is isobutanol, with a boiling point of 226.4°F, butanol at 244.4°F, 1-butanol at 262.4°F, and isoamyl at 267.8°F. There are also all kinds of esters of fatty acids, terpenes, furfurals, acetals, carboxylic acids, and aldehydes. All these materials are by-products of fermentation and important flavor carriers in every beer and wine. The concentration and composition differ depending on the type, so that we find more fermentation by-products in wheat beer than in a pilsner. Officially, up to 0.1% fusels are allowed in a distillate. These are also especially desired in whiskey and brandy, and contribute to the overall aroma. However you might want to handle your distillation, the feints certainly do not pose any threat to you.

> **NOTE** | Proportions
>
> I have already mentioned several times that the quantities to be cut are really small. Above all, if you only work with 0.5 liter tabletop stills you have little to fear. There are only a few drops—a maximum of a thimbleful—even if you distill out fresh fruit mashes. This is followed by the heart, which can vary in amount depending on the alcohol content of your base, and which you should cut at a distillation temperature of about 197.6°F. Strictly speaking, a thermometer is unnecessary for such small stills; you can simply break off the distillation when the alcoholic percentages become significantly lower, while the distillate becomes increasingly dull and tastes soapy. You can then ignore the feints, or if you wish, distill it further separately from the heart and distill it again for later use, thereby purifying it further.

Double Distilling

I will now show you how you can use double distillation to quickly distill larger quantities halfway. We are still distilling wine, but this time the aim is not "using up the leftovers," but a bottle of good brandy, which we can then age and refine. Double distilling makes the brandy altogether smoother and rounder. When tasting a freshly distilled brandy, we can't

Even more feints that are of little interest to us.

Now it gets efficient . . .

help judging it as "harsh" and "unpalatable." A friend once said he might use it to clean engines, but would not want to drink it. Many of the more disagreeable sub-flavors disappear in double distillation, which is why for some brandies, "double" or even "triple distilling" is also printed as a quality mark on the label.

Raw Spirit or Low Wine

You can simply distill off the raw spirit on the side . . .

We start with so-called raw spirit or low wine, filling our still as full as possible with wine and adding a drop of defoamer for safety. This additive, which is mainly made of silicone and is harmless, spreads over the surface of the wine and prevents it from foaming over when boiling. Thanks to this we can fill the still even up to four-fifths higher, depending on the design. Try it in a first distillation, and if the system boils over, break it off and try again with a smaller quantity. It is useful to know your own still and its maximum possible filling amount to avoid unnecessary cleaning and work, but at the same time to be able to distill the largest possible quantity.

Just let it run . . .

The distillation itself runs smoothly. You can let the entire distillate trickle directly into a larger container without having to worry about foreshots or feints. Just keep distilling until the distillate tastes tepid[19] and stop the process. As soon as you can safely open the still, empty the boiler and refill it with wine and a drop of silicone defoamer. Repeat this process several times until you have distilled all your wine stock (or your fruit mash). In all, you will need less than an hour per running. If you are ready to sacrifice a weekend to this, you can safely distill through five to ten liters of wine, even if you only use a 0.5-liter system. Keep all the results of this first distillation in a container full of so-called raw spirit or low wine. Perhaps a total of two liters of an approximately 30% ABV, roughly distilled alcohol, that still contains all the contaminants. Due to the high alcohol content, it is unlikely to spoil. After the work is done, you can set aside the raw spirit and process it further to a good fine spirit another day.

---

[19] If your still has a mounted thermometer, you can also distill by temperature and stop the operation at about 203°F.

The same process also works with all other "spirits" that you can make from fruit wine or mash. You can also process grain mashes or beer you prepared this way. As a rule, almost all brandies are traditionally double distilled. First, because relatively large quantities can be processed relatively conveniently; second, because the time for distilling can be easily arranged after the mashing, fermenting, and raw spirit distillation[20]; and third, because you will certainly obtain a good degree of purity in the alcohol by the second distillation and the entire distillate will readily reach 60% ABV after the final fine distillation. This should be possible even in very simple stills without additional dephlegmators or columns. If you do not want to rely on your sense of taste, you can also distill based on quantity systems. As a rough rule of thumb, simply distill out half the amount you have previously poured into the boiler. If you have 400 ml in the boiler, distill out 200 ml before stopping. You can also prevent the still from boiling dry this way.

. . . the ideal method for all brandies

Distill out half the boiler contents!

Fine Spirit

To distill a fine spirit, fill the still with the roughly distilled raw spirit described above and heat your boiler as usual. If you have a good temperature control on your burner you can quickly heat up to about 149°F, but then you should lower the temperature. Generally, it is better to heat over a low flame because it then takes longer for the temperature to rise and the finer foreshots alcohols that become fluid sooner will dissolve out of the raw spirit over a longer time and can evaporate through the swan neck. It is best to collect the first drops in small glasses until you are sure you have generally cut out the foreshots. Then carefully distill out the fine heart until the aroma is tepid and dull, or, if you have a thermometer, up to 197.6°F vapor temperature.

Heat over a low flame . . .

---

[20] Fruit is usually harvested in autumn and then mashed and fermented within a few days. There is often no time to distill it further. A mash can keep for a while, but it is better to distill it after resting for fourteen days. On the other hand, you can store the raw spirit almost indefinitely. Traditionally, the fine spirit is distilled during the quiet winter days and the warmth is used to heat the hut at the same time, but only if you are using an appropriately large distillery.

You will get
up to 200 ml
per run

Theoretically, you can distill 400 ml of a raw spirit with a roughly estimated 30% ABV alcohol. By calculation, this should contain 120 ml of pure alcohol. Our total result after the distillation should come out to about 60% ABV to ensure the ideal blend of purity and aroma. After the distillation, we aerate the distillate with oxygen to remove sulfur residues and dilute it with a good filtered or distilled water until we measure 38% to 40% ABV. This should yield about 200 ml per run. According to this rough calculation, after five distillations we will be able to fill a 1 liter bottle—or by working hard over a weekend, make three to five liters and thus fill a small cask.

Simple Distilling with a Dephlegmator

Distill higher
proof alcohol with
a dephlegmator.

There is still another way to obtain larger quantities or higher percentages by volume (in a weekend). With small stills, we can also work with a so-called rectifier or dephlegmator. As we learned while describing different still designs, it is enough to put a few stones in the way of the ascending vapor—the camel and donkey beasts of burden in our pictorial representation. This also works with tabletop stills if the design allows it. As soon as we have a column or an aroma chamber, we can fill it with the appropriate "stones" and make things really hard for our beasts of burden, thus, our vapor. At the same time, we could actually use real stones, but these would block the vapor route too much, which is why we should use more appropriate materials. For large systems I usually recommend just stacking schnapps or whiskey glasses, but this is not possible with tabletop stills due to their limited dimensions. For small systems, we should seriously look for something more appropriate to get the desired effect even in this small space.

Raschig Rings

We know these from the laboratory, where we sometimes fill meter-high columns with them to get extreme cleaning and dephlegmator effects. What is normal in the laboratory can also provide good service for hobbies and lead to the best results. Raschig rings are short pieces of glass, ceramic, or metal tubes that can be purchased in different diameters from laboratory suppliers. Due to the shape, you can fill any vapor chamber without blocking the passage for the vapor. The smaller the diameter of the ring, the higher the dephlegmator effect. Here you should not go too far; for hobby distilling, a six- to eight-millimeter diameter is just right. We can further modify the dephlegmator effect by the amount of rings we insert. In a 0.5-liter column still, it is possible to fill the entire column up into the head and then distill extremely high-proof alcohol, up to 80% ABV in the first run. With an Arabia tabletop still, as well as most other systems with an infusion basket, the vapor chamber can be filled so that you can use the system to rectify alcohol.

Copper Wool

Copper wool is another way to fill the area above the boiler. Similar to steel wool, copper wool consists of the finest fibers and can be easily adapted to the shape and clamped in if necessary. In contrast to raschig rings, copper wool can also be put in the head of a normal still. You should be careful not to clog the fine swan neck. You must always be sure that the vapor can still permeate through so that no unnecessary pressure builds up during distillation. You should make it harder for the vapor, but not impossible. You can test whether the still will still draw with copper wool in the head by sucking in air with your mouth through the cold swan neck. Without an attached boiler, you should still be able to effortlessly draw air through the filled head. With the boiler attached, you can also check for leaks this way. Suck the air out, then feel from the pressure whether the kettle remains leak proof, or if fresh air is flowing in and there is a leak somewhere. Be careful not to inadvertently inhale the fine copper wool or other foreign particles that may be suspended in the swan neck.

Working with copper wool offers a further advantage for distilling alcohol. By increasing the surface area where the alcohol vapor comes into contact with copper you will neutralize more hydrogen sulfides and thus achieve a smoother flavor when distilling brandy.

Copper mesh is a fine lattice plaited from copper wires that performs good service for distilling. For one, it can help in the usually coarse-grained infusion basket, so you can distill fine herbs by vapor, but you can also clamp it in the head of the still or insert it in several layers for rectifying. Copper mesh can be cut to shape and bent easily, and can be clamped in the right place due to its "wiry" quality, such as for making a protective screen in front of the swan neck.

Raschig rings made of steel, ceramic, and glass.

Sucking test: Is the column still drawing air?

The secret tip: copper wool.

Stainless Steel

The difficult choice of which stones should lie in the way . . .

Screws or nuts made of stainless steel could theoretically be used, but in such a small still they do not have the same efficiency as the items previously presented for potential ways to optimize distillation.

In the end, it is all the same how we lay the "stones" in the way of our transport column. This can be done through the design of a still to some extent—as with a reflux still, with thin, tall copper tubes; or with vapor columns, where the "Caribbean" still, with its lateral columns, would achieve the greatest effect; or just by how you fill it, where you have the choice, depending on the purpose, of filling the still to different levels and thus changing the dephlegmator effect as desired.

Our goal in distilling brandy is about 60% ABV for the finished result. You will soon get an appropriate sense of your equipment and figure out what is the optimal filling level for the still. After two or three different distillations using different filling levels, you will know what works best for your purposes and can routinize distilling your brandy in a single run. In terms of calculations, you change the results considerably with the rectification process, since you are distilling, as in the first described simple distillation, "just" 10% ABV wine, but with a 20% higher percentage result. The amounts you will get for each distillation

The solution if your beer does not taste good: distill beer schnapps!

are at least one-third lower. You must not forget to cut the foreshots and the feints during each distillation. In total, you will need a little more time for the same amount of ready-to-drink alcohol and will distill out a smaller amount than when double distilling, because you should remain watchful throughout this process, and because you may like to stop the distillation earlier due to the intense rectification. Otherwise, the same applies as described. After distillation, aerate your alcohol with oxygen and distill the distillate down to 38% or 40% ABV.

Smaller quantities than with "double distilling."

NOTE   Drinking strength

In commercial distilleries, not only do they often distill high-proof alcohols, but they also age them. A fine whiskey, cognac, or tequila is often aged at 60% ABV, and in some cases at up to 70% ABV. Brandy is already distilled to more than 80% ABV, and grain spirits to 85% ABV. Multiply distilled vodkas get up to 90% ABV, and even when distilling fruit schnapps, we go up to 60% ABV. When we are appreciating a high-proof alcohol, it is usually "only" between 38% and 42% ABV, because we can taste it best at this alcohol content. In fact, the "sharpness" of an even higher proof alcohol would at some point—at most 50% ABV—strain our taste buds so much that we would hardly be able to taste the subtleties in the flavor. It is therefore advisable to reduce the amount of alcohol with a good water. For this, we use an alcohol meter with an accurate measuring range. Appropriate alcohol meters with ranges between 30% and 60% ABV have been found to be optimal. Pour the alcohol to be measured into a sufficiently large container and slowly and carefully add water until you reach your desired range. For hobby distilling, it is recommended to reduce the alcohol to 38% ABV, not only because of the aroma, but also to "stretch" the quantity out a bit more. After all, it is two percent more if we are aiming at 38% ABV and do not adjust it to 40% or even 42% ABV, as is often typical.

We speak of drinking strength for good reason.

An alcohol meter provides useful service when adjusting to the right percentages.

IMPORTANT | Adding water

Of the right water . . .

It is important to know that adding water can and will make clear alcohol cloudy. At the same time, a glass-clear brandy shows its quality. Cloudiness is often rather undesirable and should be avoided. The cloudiness comes from the minerals and other substances contained in the water. In most distilleries, they use distilled water for mixing. As with beer, water is also an important flavor carrier. In Scotland, the fine whiskey being aged in barrels is purposefully mixed with aromatic moor water just before it is enjoyed to create special aroma experiences that match the smoky notes of the whiskey. It is best to try out in small quantities how well your water agrees with your home-distilled alcohol. I have had good experiences with our very good water in Germany's Rhön region if I run it through a water filter beforehand.

Distill or filter the water?

To the rescue: put it in the freezer with activated carbon!

If your brandy still gets cloudy, you can cool it down in the refrigerator or freezer for a few days after adding a spoonful of activated carbon, then let it run through a fine pleated filter. This is a process also used for vodka to further neutralize and moderate the aroma. The activated carbon reliably removes most of the rather unpleasant extra and abnormal flavors, thus contributing to a much more harmonious overall impression. This is a process that also works well for homemade fruit or wine brandies.

If you have followed along so far then you are in a position to distill any type of alcohol. The distillation is always the same. You can use the three methods described to distill brandy in the same way as any other *Branntwein* (spirits).[21]

Depending on the base you use for distilling, the alcohol content, and thus, the amount will vary accordingly. Depending on how much aroma you want to get from the base you will distill to a higher or lower proof level. For a clear vodka or grain spirit, you should distill to as high a proof as possible; for a flavorful fruit schnapps, leave it at 60% ABV—that is the secret.

Brandy is not the same as spirits or liquor!

Here apple and yeast are infused in honey.

---

[21] According to EU ordinance, *Branntwein* is defined as liquor with more than 37.5% ABV alcohol. The text of the law recognizes forty-six different categories. One of these is brandy (*Weinbrand* in German), which is made from wine.

Mashing and Making Alcohol

Your own mash: Small quantities do not like to ferment . . .

Making alcohol in small quantities itself is unfortunately somewhat more difficult, because quantities that are too small do not like to ferment, and also do not do so very reliably. Beyond this, the package sizes for yeasts and ingredients for hobby distilling mostly come in standard amounts of twenty-five or fifty liters. These would normally be reasonable quantities if the boilers of our legal stills did not have to be so small. It is convenient to work with the twenty-five-liter size because the containers can be moved and cleaned without too much effort. Besides, you will usually get good results because the quantities and equipment are optimally coordinated with each other. However, to distill the entire twenty-five liters at the end of a successful fermentation would indeed demand a bit too much. Distilling down a twenty-five-liter mash requires at least sixty distillations in a 0.5-liter still, if you calculate very generously and your still is a little bit bigger. This is probably too much of a good thing, even for the most persistent hobby distiller; I do not even want to think about processing a fifty-liter mash. Nevertheless, we should make friends with rather "large" quantities. Your mash should be at least five liters, because anything less really does not like to ferment, and the risk of a faulty fermentation increases significantly. You are doing yourself a big favor if you prefer to make too much and do not distill it later. Perhaps you can make a fruit wine from the rest of your mash and bottle it for later distillations or enjoy it separately. This is better than preparing a mash that is too small, which then does not want to ferment properly and develops too many contaminants and unpleasant secondary flavors.

TIP | Optimal quantity

I recommend you set the quantities between eight and twenty-five liters and buy the necessary basic equipment. Note that the fermentation tanks should also be significantly larger than the quantity of mash that you want to prepare in them to prevent them from frothing over.

CHECKLIST | Basic equipment for making alcohol

☐ Fermentation tank with a wide opening (ten to thirty liters)
☐ Fermentation lock
☐ Mash paddle
☐ Sterilizing agent (sulfur)
☐ pH test strips
☐ Acid to lower the pH value (lactic acid [80%–100%], fruit acid concentrate)
☐ Drain spigot, ladle, or wine siphon
☐ Yeast (live cultures, dry selected yeast, or turbo yeast)
☐ Thermometer (universal, infrared, or floating)
☐ Immersion blender

Additional items for making grain/potato mashes

☐ Boiler with temperature control (automatic canning kettle, Speidel's Braumeister)
☐ Thermometer (accurate measuring range from 122°F to at least 176°F)
☐ Malt or enzymes
☐ Iodine test

We know different ways to produce alcohol as hobby distillers, and fortunately all of them are legal. The law appears to be more generous about producing alcohol than about purifying the alcohol later by distillation. Beer, mead, cider, and wine (also fruit wine) are the alcoholic drinks we all know and have been able to sometimes produce for millennia. In addition, I would like to mention the distilling mash, which is specially designed for distillation of fruit brandies and is made in a way very similar to that for fruit wine. Basically, alcohol production is based on the activity of yeast cultures that absorb sugar and release alcohol. This sounds very simple at first, and works well if you take some care with your yeasts. Make sure your yeasts are healthy, because then they will gladly fall on the sugar in your mash and completely transform it into alcohol.

Beer, wine, and mash may be produced legally!

Yeast Know-How

It is important to know the differences among individual yeast varieties and understand what a yeast can and cannot do. With the right understanding of what your yeast needs to flourish, you will certainly succeed in preparing the right mash as a "habitat" for your yeasts.

Yeasts are the master distiller's friends.

Yeasts are tiny microorganisms that cannot be seen with the naked eye—more exactly, fungi. There are more than 700 yeast varieties, which, like bacteria and other microorganisms, inhabit the surface of the earth. They have been responsible for alcoholic fermentation and as a rising agent in baking since ancient times. It was Louis Pasteur who first proved in the nineteenth century that it is really yeasts that cause fermentation.[22] Before this, people left their mashes to natural and rather accidental spontaneous fermentation by wild yeasts, which are unfortunately slowly becoming extinct. This worked well for thousands of years. Even today, we still partly rely on spontaneous fermentation by natural yeast strains in fruit brandy distilleries and "old" wineries. Stone fruits and grapes offer the optimal habitat for alcohol-producing wine yeasts. Grapes and fruit are already populated with yeast fungi before they are harvested. When mashing to make fruit brandy, the pH is relatively low (optimally at about 3.5), which is very accommodating for yeasts. They can multiply quickly, and other yeast cultures or bacteria have almost no chance in the fight to become the "majority" in the mash barrel.

Look out for a low pH!

---

[22] In the Bavarian purity law for beer yeast is still not mentioned.

Adding the "living" yeast culture to the mash.

Should You Buy a Pure Yeast Culture?

For spontaneous fermentation, it is necessary to have collected the correct yeasts in sufficient quantities by chance. In a hundred-year-old wine cellar or in a wooden wine press that has been used for generations, you can still easily discover the right yeasts. In the sterile world of plastic and stainless steel tanks most yeast strains are already extinct, or are only present in small quantities. In addition, under the best conditions there is the risk of a faulty fermentation. Even with an uncomplicated wine special pure yeast cultures have been used since the 1960s. With grain mashes for grain spirits, whiskey, vodka, or beer, the risk of a faulty fermentation is even higher. The pH value is clearly above that which would be optimal for alcohol yeasts.

A pure yeast culture, as the name implies, is bred "purely" for a specific purpose. It is the best yeast for your mash, because you can be sure that from the very beginning you have sufficient amounts of exactly the right yeasts in your mash. This gives you a good feeling and guarantees a high yield.

A yeast optimized for alcohol works better than baker's yeast, but . . .

You can always ferment your mash with any commercial yeast. If you have nothing else at hand, you can also use a baker's yeast. This works, but you will soon realize that you achieve a better result with a pure yeast culture when making alcohol. In legal distilling, we should try to increase the alcohol yield from the beginning to achieve a better outcome.

Live Cultures

Live yeast cultures for fine and varietal fruit brandies and wines.

Normally, I would advise using a live culture to make your own distilling mash at home, despite the more complicated handling. Live yeast cultures are optimally bred for all sorts of different fruit varieties and uses, and are the best choice for fermenting fresh fruit so that you can distill it. They need a longer time, but create highly aromatic mashes.

Live yeast cultures are relatively sensitive and should ideally be stored in a refrigerator; too high temperatures can kill the yeast even before they are added. To be completely sure of having a "living" yeast strain, it is advisable to first start cultivating a small batch in a bottle. To do this, mix about fifty grams of sugar with half a liter of apple or grape juice in a bottle and let it stand for a day or two, until it is really fermenting. Now you can be sure and add the bottle contents to your mash.

Dry Yeast

It is easier to deal with dry selected yeast. These are dried yeasts that become active only after being added to the mash. In this case it is also a good idea to start the activation beforehand in a bottle for an optimized application. If you do not want to make so much effort, you can also stir the dry yeast directly into the mash. The yeast becomes active within a short period of time, and for smaller quantities of fruit and mash you may also mix in more yeast than the manufacturer recommends.

Turbo Yeast

Third, we love turbo yeasts for hobby distilling. Actually, a turbo yeast is also just a dry selected yeast, but it is delivered directly in a bag with a perfectly matched yeast food, guaranteeing a very fast and high-proof fermentation process and reducing the risk of a faulty fermentation. Turbo yeast is available in different versions for fruit and grain mashes, as well as for making neutral and high-proof alcohol from sugar water.

While fermenting . . .

Making a mash with turbo yeast always succeeds!

    I mentioned that I would "normally" recommend a live yeast culture for a fine brandy lovingly made from fresh fruit (and for your own wine). In the hobby area, especially when working with small tabletop stills, we are dependent on a higher alcohol content. Even if we prepare a really small mash (five liters), a fast fermentation is preferable. In addition, your mash's keeping time increases because of the higher alcohol content. With a turbo yeast, you therefore have more time to store the mash and distill it off.

TIP	Application areas

If you are in a hurry, or you want to be sure that your mash is successful—even if you are making something very high proof or aromatic—then an appropriately optimized turbo yeast would be the best choice. I would also advise turbo yeast for whiskey, grain spirits, or vodka. Because of its uncomplicated properties, turbo yeast is also ideal for beginners.

Typical glass carboy for making mash at home.

Competition

The life of the
yeasts: a
unique fight!

The yeasts in your mash are exposed to constant competition with other microorganisms. By adding specific yeast cultures we give our yeast an edge, because it is present in sufficient quantity from the start. Nevertheless, the "competitors" are not simply doing nothing, and we have to make sure that our yeasts prevail and win this almost unseen fight. The best way to do this is to offer the alcohol yeast exactly what they need. This is a little more difficult in small quantities than in a barrel containing several hundred liters, because the surfaces, and thus the possible impurities, increase. We should thus work more carefully in the small range and pay attention to the following points.

What Do Yeasts Love? Moderate Climate

This is how we can help our yeasts . . .

First of all, we should be mindful of the right climate for all yeasts and fermentations. Yeasts become inactive and work slowly at low temperatures. If the temperature is too high, the yeasts will die. Even slightly elevated temperatures would be an incubator for various bacteria that we do not want in the mash.

IMPORTANT	Be mindful of the temperature

Be sure to check the optimum temperature of your mash before adding the yeast. Fruit harvested at daybreak might be too cold. A sugared grain mash that is 161.6°F, as well as a sugar mash dissolved in boiling water, is certainly too hot. Your yeast would die immediately.

Optimal conditions: temperature as constant as possible.

If possible, the temperature should not change during the entire fermentation process. Take this into consideration when choosing your storage location. Depending on the type of yeast, the ideal temperature may be different. For pure yeast cultures, optimal temperatures are usually between 60.8° and 69.8°F. Turbo yeasts tolerate higher temperatures, sometimes up to over 86°F. In colder seasons or climates special cold fermenting yeasts can be used, which remain active at temperatures as low as 44.6°F.

The Right pH Value

I would strongly advise you to measure the pH value. Why? Well, alcohol yeasts tolerate low pH levels, but bacteria and wild yeasts do not. For this reason, you should know the pH of the mash and reduce it to between 3 and 3.5 by adding an acid. The yeasts can then continue to develop unimpeded, but the unwelcome competition will not be able to prevail.

You can determine the pH value of a mash cost effectively and reliably if you use pH measuring strips or litmus paper. Alternatively, you can buy a refractometer to determine the pH value. By carefully adding acid, you can lower the measured pH value down to a value of three. The industry mainly works with sulfuric acid, which I would not recommend. Use a more natural and appetizing acid available from normal foods.

Very simple: measuring the pH value.

You can just simply use lemon juice, but you should also know the downside. Citric acid is converted into flavors together with the fruit mash, and the acid content therefore decreases during the course of the fermentation. For an optimal result, you must check it regularly and add more acid as needed. This in turn could make it easier for bacteria to land in the mash, because you would need to open the container and stir it frequently. On the other hand, lactic acid is retained in the mash and can permanently lower the pH value. There are all sorts of other acid preparations available from suppliers especially for mashing.

Interesting to know: Citric acid is degraded, lactic acid remains!

Yeasts Love Sugar!

Of course, this is what mashing is about. Yeasts love sugar and are supposed to turn it into alcohol for us. The higher the sugar content of your mash, the higher the alcohol yield will be. Use only fully ripe fruit, then you will have much more sugar in the mash and achieve the best basic conditions for a high alcohol content and the best possible fruit flavors. As a private user, you are free to add sugar to indulge your yeasts

No yeast can resist sugar.

The best method: dissolve the sugar beforehand!

and get a higher yield. To do this, boil the sugar with water (or juice) until it has completely dissolved and let this syrup cool completely before stirring it into your mash. Remember, yeasts die immediately if you stir in the sugar mixture when it is hot!

> **NOTE** Sweetening
>
> In commercial distilleries, sweetening is prohibited because the result would be higher proof and the calculation base for taxation would be falsified. In the private sphere we can do as we like, and adding sugar to distilling mashes is really useful because of the small quantities that we can distill.

Here we add turbo yeast.

Good Nutrition

Otherwise, like all living things yeasts thrive with good nutrition; yeasts like to be "fed." With turbo yeasts, the right vitamins and minerals are right there in the bag. If you mash fruit and ferment it with a pure yeast culture (whether dry or living), you should potentially add some vitamin B6 for a faster start to the fermentation and yeast nutrient salts (for details see the packaging information) for an optimized fermentation process.

The Oxygen Problem!

Unfortunately, yeasts not only love sugar, but also oxygen; a problem that cannot be underestimated when mashing small quantities. If oxygen is present, the yeasts fall on it, "inhale" it, and neglect the conversion of sugar into alcohol. Therefore, we should try to keep the mash as acidic as possible, so that the yeasts can devote themselves to making alcohol.

Avoid oxygen!

What can we do? Close your mash container as tightly as possible and put a fermentation lock on it. A fermentation lock allows excess pressure and gases to escape from the mash barrel, but oxygen or microorganisms from the air cannot enter the container. Nevertheless, it is a good idea to carefully stir several times with a clean mash paddle at the start of fermentation. To do this, cautiously open the mash barrel and stir it around slowly without stirring oxygen into the mash if possible. If a so-called pomace cap has formed from floating fruit pieces and froth, you may also carefully stir it under. Avoid stirring it too hard, and if possible, moving the container around. The liquid inside would slosh around and oxygen would unnecessarily get mixed into the mash.

TIP	Golden Rules of Mashing

We can significantly improve the alcohol content and the quality of the flavors contained in our mash if we fulfill three simple basic prerequisites:

Three basic principles that we should know!

1. First of all, the quality of the fruit. If possible, use freshly harvested fruit that is completely ripe. Use only fruit you would eat, and remove all unappetizing spots.
2. Working hygienically is the second basic prerequisite for an error-free fermentation process. A fine aroma will only arise if there is a perfect fermentation process by the alcohol yeasts. Working cleanly prevents faulty flavors due to acetic acid or other bacteria, as well as from wild yeasts. Take care that all containers, measuring instruments, and the mash paddle are always kept clean and ideally sterilized before each use.
3. Third, watch the temperature during mashing and fermentation. Depending on the type of yeast, optimum temperatures may vary. Do not add your yeasts to the hot mash too soon (it is especially important to let starchy mashes cool down).

Take note of these three points when mashing, so you can soon distill a superb aromatic fine brandy. Remember: Only what you add in terms of quality can come out again. Mash with the best quality fine and fresh fruit and you get the finest flavor. If, on the other hand, you work in quantity, then you can also add lower quality pieces. But you should know that any piece of rotten fruit will avenge itself, not only in the taste, but also in the quantity of the poisonous foreshots, which we actually want to avoid.

Practical work with an immersion blender.

Practical Mash Making

First, I recommend you wash your fruit right after it is harvested, for example, washing it with a hose. Pip fruits, such as apples or quinces, may be kept at room temperature briefly to develop a fuller aroma. Depending on the type of fruit, the material should then be crushed. With more delicate fruit, you have to weigh each case and make appropriate compromises. Berries are especially delicate, and depending on the amount and how firm the fruit is, you have to decide whether you prefer to do without washing or warming.

Pip Fruits

Hard fruit should be crushed before mashing!

With hard pip fruits such as apples, quinces, or pears, it is a good idea to use a fruit mill to process the crop quickly and uniformly. The advantage is that relatively large quantities can be processed and macerated at the same quality. You can mash whole pip fruits, making the processing relatively uncomplicated, and this also works well for beginners. On the whole, pip fruits are very suitable for distilling schnapps. Pears give off more flavors than apples or quinces. With Williams pears, it is a good idea to remove the stems beforehand, since these can overlay the fine aroma. The ideal temperature for mashing pip fruits is below 69.8°F.

Here I am adding lactic acid to the mash to lower the pH value.

Stone Fruits

You should not use a normal fruit mill to crush stone fruits such as cherries, plums, apricots, or peaches. You have to work more carefully so that the stones (pits) are not damaged. Stone fruit pits contain amygdalin, which breaks down into hydrogen cyanide when it comes into contact with water. Hydrogen cyanide is a deadly poison you certainly do not want in your mash. Hydrogen cyanide breaks down only inside a pit and in combination with water. Just make sure you do not damage any of the pits. Besides, up to five percent of the pits may be inadvertently damaged by processing before you need to worry. If you use a machine, use a mill with rubber rollers, then most of the pits stay in one piece. Most stone fruits are softer than pip fruits and do not necessarily have to be crushed beforehand; crushing the fruit is often enough.

With some fruit, you just have to crush them coarsely by hand.

If you want to be completely safe, remove the pits before mashing. For apricots, plums, or peaches, this should not be a problem if you can get a little loving assistance from your family. For hobby distilling, removing the pits from a home-prepared mash is almost spiritual work and certainly strengthens the emotional bond to your fine brandy. Nevertheless, you should know that the pits also contribute to the bouquet of some drinks. Especially with cherry brandy, and sometimes with Italian plums, you should leave a few pits in the mash to preserve the typical slightly bitter, almond-like flavor which in part enriches stone fruit brandies. Stone fruit mashes tolerate temperatures of up to 77°F without compromising quality.

Important: With stone fruits, remove the pits or leave them whole!

Berries

Wine grapes are particularly productive and easy to process. You should pick over berries such as currants, rowan berries, or elderberries, which can lead to a lot of work. For most berry varieties, the yield is unfortunately too low to make a mash. Because berries often contain less sugar or enzymes, this can slow down the fermentation process, and you have to calculate even more disadvantages when making a mash. In addition, some varieties (such as strawberries) are reluctant to yield their aroma to the alcohol. It is therefore often advisable to steep berries in a high-proof alcohol to distill off the alcohol later. Here too, you have to decide how many berries you have available in what quality, and if you want to make a mash from them, or rather a *Geist*. Berries should also be crushed or ground during mashing, and if possible fermented at temperatures below 69.8°F.

Slightly more difficult: making a berry mash.

Starchy Bases

Grain mashes: a bit more complicated, but always worth it . . .

With starchy bases such as grains or potatoes, we have to perform an additional step. It is not enough to simply crush the potatoes or the grain; we must convert the contained starch into sugar before we add the yeast. This is done by adding malt or enzymes and keeping the mash at certain temperatures (143.6°F and 161.6°F) over a longer period of time so that the enzymes can work. In hobby distilling, automatic canning machines work very well; you can use them to conveniently prepare up to twenty liters of grain mash in one step. Beer brewing machines, such as the Speidel Braumeister, also work very well. Beer brewing is very similar to the preparation of a mash for whiskey, vodka, or grain spirits.

IMPORTANT | Be mindful of the temperature

It is important to wait until the mash has completely cooled after converting the starch into sugar. Just as fresh fruit can be too cold in the autumn, a grain mash might be too hot and your yeast might die.

Sugar Mash

Turbo yeast and sugar mash.

Perhaps this method seems a bit radical, but sugar water works very well for making a high-proof alcohol as a base for subsequent use. In combination with turbo yeast, you can very quickly and efficiently make a neutral alcohol for a base for all kinds of experiments, or for further processing into liqueurs and *Geists*.

First, stir the sugar or molasses into five liters of boiling hot water until it has completely dissolved. Depending on the type of yeast, the amounts may vary; it is best to read the information on the package and use the total amounts indicated. My personal "recipe" deviates from the package information somewhat because I first dissolve the sugar in a partial amount of water. This is an important step, since with this method the yeasts are able to process a pre-prepared sugar syrup better than solid sugar crystals. By boiling it, we guarantee the mash is free of germs and a complete and even distribution of the sugar in the water. When everything is safely dissolved, we add the remaining water and check the temperature of the mixture. This should be less than 86°F, so that the yeast does not die due to a temperature that is too high. Please note the manufacturer's instructions. With the right yeast, you can ultimately obtain an alcohol that is up to 20% ABV within five days.

Due to their high alcohol content, fully fermented grain mashes will keep for a very long time if you simply store them in a cool place after the fermenting is finished. Also turbo yeast varieties are very convenient for us hobby distillers. You can easily prepare twenty-five liters of sugar alcohol at once and then process it as needed. If you want to make smaller quantities, the risk of a faulty fermentation is also very low. Just use half the amount called for in the package information for making twelve liters, or buy smaller packets of turbo yeast for only eight liters of mash.

Dissolving sugar in hot water.

Typical must cask with accessories for making a mash.

> ### NOTE Use large containers
>
> On most turbo yeast packages, it also calls for using an open container without a fermentation lock for fermenting the mash due to the intense foaming and fermentation. An approach I would not recommend in any case. Instead, use a sufficiently large container and an equally large-sized fermentation lock. The Speidel must casks work very well, because these come with a large seventeen-millimeter-thick fermentation lock that can be easily cleaned.

Fermentation

With a little practice, you can quickly learn to make mash. The actual principles are always the same, no matter what yeasts or starting materials we use. If you know your yeasts and fruits, then you can quickly achieve remarkable results and create small aroma miracles.

Experiment: Making a mash of canned fruit.

As a rule, it is sufficient for the fruit to be coarsely ground or crushed under basic hygienic conditions into clean (previously sterilized) fermentation tanks. The finer you crush and prepare the mash, the easier it is for the yeasts to convert the sugar into alcohol later, and thus produce aromas. For berries and watery fruits, I would recommend using an immersion blender to ensure a steady and certain fermentation process. Some fruits develop a fuller bouquet by slowing the action of the yeasts. You can also use turbo yeasts when fermenting fruit, which I would recommend for beginners. In this case, you will need significantly less yeast. A mini packet is enough for twenty-five liters, and the normal packages can ferment up to one hundred liters of fruit mashes. For safety reasons, you should measure temperature before the yeast is added. Most "normal" yeasts work optimally between 57.2° and 68°F. At lower temperatures, use a special cold fermentation yeast; use turbo yeast when working at higher temperatures.

When mashing, always watch the temperatures!

Generally, a slow fermentation is preferred when making aromatic fruit mashes for distilling fine fruit brandies. At higher temperatures the fermentation goes faster, but for the bouquet at the end of the fermentation it is better to let the aroma develop a little longer. Warmer temperatures are also a playground for all kinds of microorganisms and bacteria, and you should avoid creating a comfortable climate for them. Certainly, you would not want your work to be for nothing and the mash to turn bad. If you expect higher temperatures, use turbo yeast. If you live in the south or do not have a basement with evenly cool temperatures, you should use turbo yeast instead of a pure yeast culture. Bacteria have no chance against the power nutrients contained in the packages that make the robust yeast strains grow rapidly. For an optimal result do without some aroma nuances, instead getting a stable and higher proof alcohol, which is clearly an advantage when distilling with a mini still.

At high temperatures, it is preferable to use turbo yeast!

Distilling Fruit Brandies

At this point you should be good at distilling and have ample experience distilling wine and beer. The basic principles are always the same, including for distilling fruit brandies from your own mash. But only the basic principles! Unfortunately, it is not that easy. Distilling a genuine fruit brandy requires a lot more sensitivity. In contrast to distilling brandy, we are now working with a real mash for the first time. Depending on what you have fermented intensely, your mash can now be relatively viscous, and maybe even jellied by the pectins, or contain all kinds of chunks and solids sloshing around if they have not already sunk to the bottom. Peels, pits, pods, whatever—we can safely conclude that a mash offers a completely different alcohol base for distilling than a fluid wine or beer, even if the alcohol content is similar.

Warning: Mash tends to burn!

Here pears are crushed by hand.

Secure the fermentation tank with a fermentation lock!

What Makes a Difference When We Distill?

When distilling mash, we must reckon with it sticking to the bottom and getting scorched very easily. This scorching, in turn, leads to an unpleasant aroma and completely unnecessary cleaning. In fact, it can be very hard to clean a scorched kettle because the opening is too small. When you buy a still, you should pay attention to whether you can order spare parts later. Finally, I would definitely advise using a copper boiler for distilling mash. Thanks to the unique material properties of copper, it will be harder for your mash to get scorched than in glass or stainless steel. Copper offers by far the best thermal conductivity, which leads to a better distribution of temperature than other materials. Beyond this, copper can be worked into perfectly round, smooth shapes, so we can often get round, bubble-shaped boilers in miniature stills, which also helps to improve heat distribution. Nevertheless, the distilling of fruit mash remains an art. In large boilers, it is already hard enough not to let the mash scorch. With tiny units heated by a single small flame at only one point, you must always calculate on the mash getting scorched on the bottom.

In large industrial distilleries, they use powerful agitators or pumping systems that keep the mash in motion during distillation. These methods are completely ruled out in our small scale. In hobby distilling, we have to protect the mash from scorching using other methods. A mash sieve works best to do this, and we can cut one out from copper mesh and bend it into shape. The purpose of a mash sieve is to keep some space between the heavier parts of the mash and the bottom of the kettle. Solid pieces cannot sink to the bottom, and a mash sieve or mash basket keeps the mash cleanly separated from the hot walls of the kettle and only lets liquids flow through.

Use a mash sieve of copper mesh at the bottom of your boiler!

In larger distilleries, they used to place some dry straw underneath, or as an alternative to copper mesh, plaited some peeled willow branches. Both methods unfortunately will not work in 0.5-liter boilers, because it would be difficult to keep the straw or the woven willow on the boiler bottom. Both would also significantly reduce the volume in the boiler. The infusion basket used by Helge Schmickl in Austria has a similar function; it is a steamer basket made of stainless steel, which in bigger stills can be easily expanded as a spacer in the boiler.

It would be just as effective to sew a fine-meshed sack, which fits as exactly as possible, from a porous fabric and fill it with the mash. This is a method that is somewhat more difficult to handle in practice, but it works well when the fabric is porous enough. Be sure to use a natural heat-resistant fabric, since you certainly do not want to let the contaminants from melted plastic get into your drink. Linen or cotton fabrics work very well.

We still have another method, which is to liquefy the mash, but this would not be the most sensible solution, given the tiny boilers and the associated restricted possibilities. It is better to squeeze out the liquid before the distillation and simply not distill the extra material in the mashes. It is not easy to filter some mashes beforehand, and this often takes a long time, but it can be quite worth it, because you no longer have to watch out during the distillation.

Many methods – one goal. Keep your mash from scorching!

A steamer basket at the bottom of the boiler as a mash sieve.

Pomace Brandies or Marcs

A basic truth about grappa: A pomace contains hardly any alcohol and therefore there is little sense in distilling it in a mini still.

It is not impossible to produce pomace brandies or marcs with a miniature still, but the quantity you can expect is really very small. Pomace is the solid remains from wine making; in our case the solid, crushed leftovers from already fermented grapes that remain behind after pressing red wine. We can fill our still with pomace, if possible up into the column, and then pour in some water. Ideally, you should also put in a small mash sieve beforehand, as pomace also tends to scorch. Heat the kettle, and the water penetrates through the grapes, mixes with the residual alcohol, and takes this along with it into the condenser. You should not expect any miracles here when distilling with a 0.5-liter still, because you cannot distill out any more alcohol than is contained in the pomace. And this as a rule is usually very little; it will be hardly more than a few droplets to taste. For experimental purposes and to learn about distilling, this is nevertheless interesting.

Apples and grapes are the easiest to work with for hobby distilling.

Grain Spirits

Distilling a mash made of a starchy base such as grain, corn, or potatoes is much simpler than distilling a fruit mash, because we remove all the malt and grain before distilling and only distill off the pure liquid. Making the mash itself is more expensive, but that should not deter us. First, making a grain mash is a lot of fun and creates interesting experiences; second, we can also brew beer using the same technique, and so use our knowledge as well as the equipment twice at the same time. I recommend you involve yourself in this topic extensively if you want to go deeper into the subject matter and want an "honest" base for your distillates.

Grain spirits: simple and difficult at the same time.

Grain spirits are often prepared so that they are lower in terms of percentage of alcohol than fruit or sugar mashes, but they can be distilled into a significantly higher proof alcohol. You can easily distill a clear alcohol as a base for making a *Geist* to more than 80% ABV later on, even if at the same time you do not have to distill it twice, but even three or four times. Think of the old alchemists, who in their time only called an alcohol "superb" after the tenth distillation—but also modern vodka distilleries, which likewise sometimes distill up to nine times in succession.

Superb distilling to over 80% ABV.

TIP	High proof results

To obtain a sufficient quantity of a high proof alcohol with a miniature still you can, as described for brandy, distill the raw spirit and fine spirit separately. It is up to you how frequently you distill an alcohol before you convert it into a fine spirit. If you want to get larger amounts of a very pure alcohol, then I recommend you buy it ready made at the pharmacy, or at least use a purchased vodka or grain spirit as a base and distill it to a higher proof. Unfortunately, legislation is not on our side . . .

Patiently distill several times in a row . . .

Concluding Words and Recommendations on Alcohol

The simple method of producing alcohol using turbo yeast in sugar water is suitable for anyone in a hurry and for beginners. To make a clear alcohol from your own fruit or grain mash, on the other hand, is in the royal class. It is not for nothing that such liquors are also called "fine brandies." These require correspondingly more love, work, and care, especially when dealing with the legal dimensions. Each step in handling such tiny dimensions increases the precious, extremely small quantities with which we work in hobby distilling. In a private setting, we enhance a fine brandy into a noble piece of ourselves, since we have earned every single bottle of it with great effort and can certainly build a special relationship with the materials, equipment, and work processes we used. If you want to produce results primarily in presentable quantities without doing a lot of work, then you should stay with making *Geist*.

Storage and Refining

We can distill, but as you have probably noticed in our experiments, a freshly distilled brandy is by no means as delicious as we would like it to be. A freshly distilled alcohol often tastes spicy or even sulfurous. The art of making a delicious liquor does not end with distilling!

Rounding and Refining

We already know a few measures and methods to harmoniously round off our drinks, but I would like to briefly differentiate between a *Geist*, which is usually made from an already finished alcohol and enhanced with flavor, and a fresh liquor in all its power. We can taste the *Geist* directly after distilling, then pass it on and bottle it. We indeed also know stored *Geist*s, but in most cases, we will enjoy this spirit with its various aromas in all its freshness. *Geist*, or spirit, is named for good reason: the

Various *Geists* and brandies.

fine aroma it contains can evaporate over the years. It is therefore also advisable to seal a fine *Geist* tightly and consume opened bottles within a year. By contrast, we can use various methods to tone down, rarefy, age, flavor, and change the color of a distilled liquor.

A *Geist* can evaporate!

Oxygen

A freshly distilled liquor profits from the addition of oxygen. Especially with brandies, it is worthwhile to aerate them intensely—depending on the amount—using a whisk, or by repeatedly shaking it vigorously in the bottle. For larger quantities, you can aerate the whole container with an aquarium air pump overnight. The oxygen removes unpleasant stinging sulfur odors and tones the liquor down significantly. Other distilled liquors also profit from "breathing," which is why I would generally recommend a homemade liquor be enriched with oxygen in the first step immediately after distillation. Small quantities may simply be left open in the refrigerator for a few days to "breathe." The method of oxygenating creates an overall smoother product and lets the aromas gathered in the alcohol emerge more clearly.

Oxygen: bad in a mash, but good in a finished liquor.

Water

As with beer, added water can act on the aroma in a liquor. They even say that for beer, water is a basic flavor carrier and responsible for the many taste differentiations among individual beer brands. This is similar for schnapps, but you can only taste the differences in the lower proof range. Depending on the drinking strength, the alcohol often overlays the fine aromas. In Scotland, whiskey is individually served with a jug of spring water, so you can adjust it to your personal drinking strength. In general, when adjusting to drinking strength, a mild, low-sodium and bicarbonate water should be used, so as not to influence the liquor aroma too strongly. In commercial distilleries, distilled water is normally used not only because this way the aroma can be attributed just to the liquor, but also because it prevents any subsequent clouding.

Water according to taste!

The minerals contained in water can flocculate when mixed with alcohol as a milky cloudiness and destroy the clear beauty of a fine liquor. Which water you choose is up to you. I personally am not disturbed by the cloudiness caused by a good spring water in my own liquors. However, if I were to produce larger quantities and wanted to bottle or give away the alcohol, I would rather mix it with a distilled, or at least filtered water to dilute the liquor to drinking strength.

Activated Carbon

Using activated carbon is underestimated, although it has long been customary in the industry to treat all kinds of liquors with carbon. As early as 1822, Friedrich Lüdersdorf described the "de-fuseling of spirits"[23] using different types of carbon, a method considered almost normal today and used as a sales argument for some spirits due to the multiple distillations. In the nineteenth century, research was done on which carbon was the most suitable; for example, that the effect increased and the cleaning effect improved when using finer charcoal from lighter woods.

Activated carbon is often underestimated.

Today, we have gone a few steps farther and can take advantage of the painstakingly collected experiences of previous generations. We know the filtering properties of carbon which is finely ground, porous, and thus contains more oxygen in various areas, ranging from aquarium filters to drinking water filters. The industry supplies the finest carbon for every purpose. Due to the inexpensive prices and the small amounts required for hobby distilling, it is hardly worthwhile to produce it ourselves. Due to the extremely fine, and at the same time porous surface of modern activated carbon, it binds the alcoholic by-products and at the same time releases oxygen into the drink. A double effect that we like to use in hobby distilling to make our beverages ready to drink within twenty-four hours.

Simple application— great effect!

Nowadays, the application is a child's game. It is enough to add a teaspoon of activated carbon to a bottle of distillate diluted to drinking strength and shake it vigorously. After letting it rest for twelve to twenty-four hours in the refrigerator, you can slowly filter your liquor through a fine filter and bottle it directly, or make a comparative tasting of the difference with an unfiltered drink. Do not leave the carbon in your drink for too long, because after a period of about twenty-four hours it

---

[23] In the book *The Essence of Art of Distilling*, published in Berlin in 1822.

can become over-saturated. The carbon will then return the secondary aromas to the drink again and your work was in vain. With the activated carbon method, if you simultaneously cool it as much as possible, you can also subsequently remove cloudiness from water that is too mineral-rich from your liquor.

Barrel Storage

Especially with whiskey and brandy, but also with rum or tequila, wood flavors often dominate due to storage in wooden barrels. With whiskey, it has become almost fashionable to create flavors with different types of wood or used barrels and to name them on the label. Think of names like "triple wood" or "double cask" to establish that the master distiller can create special flavors just by storing the liquor in certain types of wood. In these two examples, the whiskeys are stored in different wooden barrels for specific times. "Port wood," "bourbon barrel," or "sherry cask"

Different woods and processing yield different flavors.

You can buy genuine wooden barrels starting at a one-liter volume.

speak for themselves, because whiskeys often gain in flavor through storage in "old" sherry, port, or bourbon barrels. A good trick to enrich a liquor, especially since used barrels take up much of the special aromas from their original use over the years and then return these to the whiskey. In particular, used sherry casks are traded for the highest prices for this reason, and hundreds are transported from southern Spain to northern England. Modern distilleries have discovered these methods for themselves, and thus we find stored grappas, vodkas, and aquavits, and lately even various fruit brandies.

To fill a barrel with your own whiskey is legally possible — but you need patience.

With the modest quantities we can make in hobby distilling, long term barrel storage is not always the best method. Fortunately, at this point, we can improvise, shorten the long time periods, and save on some of the equipment. According to the law, a real whiskey must age for at least three years in a wooden barrel. Without these three years it would be just a simple grain spirit. In Spain, they are open to you making your own wine or brandy, and you can buy very small, genuine sherry casks. To make an officially approved whiskey, you might want to get such a fine barrel of American white oak, fill it with a sherry or port wine to wash it out, and then store your own whiskey for three years (or longer).

Barrel Know-How

Proper storage is an important basic building block for the later aroma in your liquor. If you really want to store your home distilled liquor in a wooden barrel, then you should know some important things beforehand.

Sealed or Open?

Relatively inexpensive sealed wooden barrels are available in the trade; these are mostly coated with paraffin inside and keep the stored liquid safely in the barrel. These barrels are more suitable for storing or dispensing alcohol, because due to the coating there is no exchange between the wood and the stored alcohol. Such barrels are excellent for storing finished alcohol if it is not supposed to change in flavor anymore. Coated barrels are as neutral to the drink as stainless steel tanks or glass bottles.

In contrast, most of the barrels consist of bare wood that has been partly burnt or charred inside. The charring creates several new chemical compounds and colors that merge into a popular woody caramel total note. In addition, the charring expands the surface, creating an "activated carbon effect" which can filter out the various low quality alcoholic aromas and by-products from the liquor. With an uncoated barrel, the exchange between the wood and the drink is a given, and depending on the type of wood and whether the barrel has been charred or not, completely different aromas are obtained.

Your distillate will only profit from a barrel of blanched or charred wood!

Which Barrel for Which Drink?

American white oak is generally regarded as the best wood for barrel storage; a wood that is used for almost all sherry and bourbon barrels due to the fine notes of vanilla. Depending on the region, you can also use other woods, such as fine French oak, which is also well suited for storing fine liquors. Since the wood notes later change the entire drink, you should absolutely pay attention to which wood you are working with. Charred oak barrels are particularly suitable for liquors that should take on a strong color and flavor. The flavor is typical of bourbon whiskeys, while French cognacs are preferably stored in barrels of French oak. Nowadays, small casks are being specially made for us hobby distillers from the wood of former sherry, bourbon, and port wine casks. If, on the other hand, you just want to lightly emphasize the actual character and color of a liquor, such as a fine fruit brandy, then you should take barrels made of less dominant ash wood or the wood of an untoasted Limousin oak. Alternatively, barrels of chestnut, cherry, or acacia are also available.

Many woods and many drinks. Which is the best?

You should also know that a cask for hobby distilling is considerably smaller than a barrel for a large distillery. Sometimes you can buy real casks starting at one or two liters! This creates a completely different relationship between the wood surface and contents. Small casks give more aroma and color to the drink than a large barrel would. The aging process is significantly accelerated. Check occasionally and pour it into a stainless steel or glass container if you have leached out enough aroma.

Important to know: Smaller casks give off more aroma and color . . .

Angels' Share and Devil's Cut

A two-percent loss per year is not a rare occurrence.

The so-called "angels' share" is a big problem for us hobby distillers. This is the portion that evaporates through the barrel walls[24] during storage and can easily be two percent per year from a large barrel. In a small cask you have to expect even higher losses. You may eventually be able to limit this evaporation somewhat by using a barrel painted on the outside or wrapping the entire barrel in foil. Then you just have to make sure that it does not get moldy . . .

The "devil's cut" is more of an advertising gag by the American whiskey industry, and in contrast to the fleeting angels' share, symbolizes the highly aromatic sediment in a whiskey barrel. No further losses are to be expected here. You can empty a small cask down to the last drop or fill up the long-stored lees with a fresh batch. Then your liquor is "blended," or mixed, and tasted. In Spain, brandies are stacked atop each other in four rows of barrels and the young brandy is filled into the topmost barrel. The contents of the barrels travel one row lower each year, and the four-year-old brandy from the lowest barrel is then mixed with the lees from the previous years and decanted for filling. Some portions in the bottom barrel can therefore be tens of years old, depending on how long the bodega (cellar) has existed. This "Solera process" is well suited for us in hobby distilling, because this way we can keep the barrels in good condition due to regular refilling and decanting, and in the course of several years look back on a fine collection of self-distilled, and at least in tiny doses, also really old stored liquors.

The Solera system: also suitable for home use?

Barrel Care

Always keep your barrel filled!

A barrel wants to be cared for, and the main thing is to keep the barrel moist. A genuine and unsealed barrel is made of loosely joined wooden staves held together by a metal ring. In dry conditions the staves can contract and fall apart—filled, they expand and solidly seal the gaps between the individual staves. It is not so easy to puzzle out how to put a dilapidated barrel back together and keep it evenly moist, but as a layman, you should try to repair it again and make it tight.

---

[24] According to a Scottish legend, this is the share that the angels approve from the barrels, hence the source of the name: the share for the angels.

> **TIP** Keep the barrels moist
>
> I recommend you regularly check your barrels and refill them if necessary. The best, of course, is with the drink you want to age in the barrel. If you are not using your barrel, you can simply fill it with water. I would recommend you use boiled water with some sulfur powder to prevent any moldiness and development of bacteria.

New barrels are sometimes delivered dry and should not dry out again after they are first filled. It is best to always rinse new barrels a few times with hot water before using them. Particularly small, charred casks should be initially treated with a "cheaper" alcohol to prevent excessively strong changes to the flavor and color of your laboriously produced fine liquors. If you want to add some special flavors to the barrel, you should store a sherry or port in it for the first year; your home distilled whiskey you fill it with later will thank you for this.

Alternative Ways to Enhance Flavor

Wood Flavors

Since we usually only have relatively small amounts of alcohol available, we can very easily imitate barrel storage by simply adding wood chips of corresponding varieties to our alcohol in a bottle. The ultimate effect— namely, coloring our distillate and making it flavorful—is the same as that of barrel storage. A bottle full of wood chips is just not as stylish as an oak wood barrel. Many different types of wood and toasted wood chips are available in the trade, especially for hobby distillers, and invite you to experiment. Handling them is child's play, and if you look around a bit in specialist magazines you will quickly find out that even commercial distillers prefer to store their liquor with oak chips in a stainless steel vat than in real wooden barrels.

Proud of your own whiskey!

Noble wood panels replace the barrel!

Just add one or two teaspoons of wood chips to your drink in a bottle and store the whole thing in a dark place at an even temperature. Your distillate will change color and aroma after just a few days, just as if it were in a wooden barrel. Perhaps you could actually endure it and age a bottle of home distilled whiskey in this way for several years? According to the law, it is then indeed not a true whiskey because it was not stored in a barrel - but who knows, and what difference does it make at home? Besides real wood chips, you can also experiment with walnut shells or edible chestnuts. What pleases you is allowed - and if it enriches your drink with aroma and color, it can only be for the good.

Caramel and Sugar

Use caramelized sugar to fiddle things, as they do in the industry!

By adding sugar and caramel, we are close to departing from the path of honest and fine liquors and ending up dangerously close to counterfeiting, or legal but simpler spirits. But honestly, why should we not use the same tricks at home as the industry does to make our drink a bit more pleasing? By law, up to three percent sugar can be added to a cognac. Besides, the color may be darkened with caramel to imitate a longer barrel storage.

In hobby distilling, we can literally blend both methods by gently heating sugar in a pan (or in a spoon) until it turns brown. You have to stir it carefully so that the sugar does not burn. When all the sugar is melted and uniformly browned, we carefully add water and stir it into a thick, sweet caramel syrup. We can mix small quantities of this into our home distilled alcohol to taste to create a brownish color, as well as to create a taste more pleasing to many tongues. Of course, this method only works for dark liquors; for clear liquors, simply dissolve light sugar in water to make a sugar syrup and add it. Especially for spicier liquors with anise, caraway, or fennel, adding a little sugar is also allowed and often even desirable. Ultimately, only your sense of taste determines what tastes best for you personally and whether you prefer to keep things a bit sweeter or more tart.

Sugar, orange juice, and brandy make a liqueur.

Essences and Flavors

Another method we know for enhancing an alcohol is to flavor it using industrially produced essences. Similar to our large-scale gin production, we simply add the finished flavoring to a neutral alcohol to transform it into our favorite drink. Depending on the type of alcohol, the flavor essences are supplied in the optimal amounts exactly fine tuned for a specific quantity. It is hard to go wrong. Most of the higher quality essences come from Sweden, where "secret" distilling seems almost to be a sport because of the high tax on brandies. Simple clear liquors are extracted from sugar water and then converted into your respective favorite drink by adding the appropriate flavoring. Thanks to the flavorings, it is possible to make any kind of liqueur or alcohol and inexpensively create a well-stocked home bar. You can also use the essences in other ways, for example, to refine a somewhat weakly flavored fruit schnapps a bit or to imitate barrel aging.

Aromatizing industrial alcohol with ready-made essences.

In addition to fully prepared liqueur, fruit brandy, gin, tequila, whiskey, and cognac flavorings, we also know of pure food flavorings from the food industry, which we can also use sparingly but effectively to give a home distilled liquor that extra something special. Here, too, we find a wide range from wood to brandy and whiskey, including various fruit flavorings and often those made from purely natural ingredients without artificial additives. Theoretically, when using purchased flavorings and essences, you can even get results without distilling at all, as long as you buy your alcoholic base in the form of inexpensive vodka or *Doppelkorn* in the nearest supermarket and mix it at home. Even then, your home-blended bottle of gin is usually even cheaper than a comparable brand. Try it; ultimately, the industry does just the same.

Improve your own liquor with purchased flavorings?

Your own schnapps without distilling!

Bottling

When your liquor is ready and you have tasted it, it is time to bottle. I like to use 0.35-liter liquor bottles with twist-off caps, but also collect other beautiful bottles all year round for reuse. Ultimately, bottling involves keeping your laboriously achieved liquor like a trophy. A fine liquor and its flavor are really honored with a beautiful bottle. Once we have decided that a mix is now perfect for our palate and those of our

acquaintances, then it is guaranteed to be a pleasure to taste it again later on and compare it. Even greater is the pleasure of having good friends or acquaintances taste your liquor, or even giving them a bottle, and then receiving appreciative approval.

The greatest fun: tasting with friends.

NOTE | Keeping quality

Fine liquors, especially those that have already been aged, can be stored for a relatively long time in a bottle without altering the flavor. Only the fine aroma of fruit brandies, if the quantity is small, can vanish within a year. Be sure to keep your bottles closed as tightly as possible and store them in a dark, evenly cool place, so you can enjoy the variety of your own liquors many years later.

Distilling Essential Oils

The distillation of essential oils differs significantly from distilling alcohol, and we should consider some things before we get down to work. When distilling alcohol, we add a base that already contains alcohol to the boiler and dissolve out the alcohols that evaporate earlier because of its lower boiling point. At the same time, the alcoholic vapor can leach out different aromas and essential oils from plants, spices, or herbs along its way through the still and carry these along with it. This process is also called *Schleppdestillation* in German (carry-along distillation), meaning a steam infusion distillation process. It does not matter whether the aromas are extracted from our plant material by steam, or after previous soaking are distilled out directly in the boiler. The alcohol combines with the aromas to form a unit and transports them safely through the cooling system to your condenser in the still. In the end, we get an alcohol enhanced with the widest range of ingredients from our material, which, according to the type of plant, is usually highly aromatic alcohol. Some of the alcohols obtained this way are so fine in aroma that resourceful stillmen and distillers even fill their fine "schnapps" into tiny bottles with atomizers and offer them as "cherry" or "pear perfume." The fragrant result is partly due to the essential oils, which are completely soluble in the alcohol. Also, or above all, making *Geist* involves taking the essential oils contained in the plant material over into our alcohol. For this reason, plants with high aromatic oil content, such as anise, juniper, caraway, or fennel, are also particularly popular and uncomplicated aroma dispensers for distilling schnapps. But we have a problem!

In This Chapter

- The Problem
- The Solution
- Practical Distillation of Essential Oils
- What Is the Best Way for Me to Distill What?
- Hydrosols

Essential oils mix inseparably with alcohol!

The Problem

Essential oils bind inextricably with alcohol! We can indeed transfer all kinds of fine flavorings into alcohol by distillation, but the essential oils can then no longer be separated from the alcohol. Remember this simple principle: Essential oils dissolve completely in alcohol! We can use this knowledge in the hobby area in many ways, in that we distill the flavorings directly with alcohol to obtain larger quantities of aromatic treats. These are not real essential oils, but good, highly aromatic and homemade bases for natural cosmetics or perfumes. On the other hand, it is possible to enhance, "stretch," and preserve pure essential oils with alcohol. Especially if you are only able to make very small amounts of essential oils, it is recommended to mix in a few drops of a neutral alcohol to increase the amount and the keeping quality. With a mixture of three parts alcohol to one part essential oils, you get four times the quantity and a considerably longer keeping quality. A little trick that is quite allowed in the private sphere and ultimately gives us presentable results that are still of the best, homemade quality. But enough on the subject of alcohol. It is time that we seriously tend to distilling essential oils.

Here the essential oil floats in a fine layer on top.

The Solution

In chemical terms alcohol is a "solution," but not the solution for making essential oils.

Actually, everything is quite simple. We do not distill our essential oils with alcohol, but with water! At the beginning of this book, we made a test distillation with water to try out our still, and thus determined that the boiling point of water is actually[25] at 212°F. We therefore need a little more energy than for distilling alcohol to heat up the still appropriately.

Very simple: We distill with water!

Water is almost always available and usually does not mix with essential oils. As a result, water is the ideal base for distilling the precious essential oils out of the plant materials we are using. If we obtain sufficient quantities, after the distillation we can separate the essential oils from the remaining herbal distillate—also known as a hydrosol, which are also made aromatic by the distillation— with a pipette. Most of the essential oils float on top and can be distinguished from the hydrosols after they are left to rest briefly.

---

[25] Depending on weather conditions and altitude.

Unfortunately, this does not apply to all of them. Clove oil sinks to the bottom, but can then be removed with a pipette. Other oils are almost invisible, and we might even need a pair of glasses or a magnifying glass, and certainly good lighting to see the fine transition when separating them out. For hobby distilling, we can work well using a fine pipette and small test tubes. I have had very good experiences with a so-called safety pipette. With these you can take up extremely small doses and need only one hand while you hold the test tube at an angle and in the right position with the other hand. Even if safety pipettes are a lot more expensive, buying one is worth it.

Before we can think about separating the essential oils from the hydrosol, we must first distill the plants whose oils we wish to preserve. And before we distill, we should be clear about expected quantities. Only about one percent of all plants contain essential oils. Some of them are very oily and can be distilled well in a mini still, including cloves, juniper, anise, fennel, caraway, mint, rosemary, thyme, and of course that friend of all distillers, lavender. With these plants, we can count on getting from a few drops to several milliliters of essential oil and an abundant yield of aromatic herbal distillate (hydrosol).

Optimal for tiny quantities: the safety pipette.

With many other plants, it is unfortunately impossible to obtain even a single drop of their precious oil in a mini still. A few years ago, for the sake of experiment, I tried to fill a thirty-liter column still with fresh rose petals gathered at dawn and distill them. In this process, I was able to see only a single drop of the essential oil floating on the herbal distillate. Jasmine or orange blossoms are similarly difficult. We should not try to distill delicate flower oils as a hobby so we can avoid a big disappointment from the start.

What we get instead of the essential oils are fine herbal distillates, also called hydrosols. In the case of rose petals, a fresh, rather "green" fragrant rose water that we can use for skin care. We can make such hydrosols on a small scale with a miniature still, as well as with a large system. The expected amounts of hydrosols are quite sufficient for us to be able to use them generously afterward.

TIP | **Find suitable plants**

To get a feeling for which plants are suitable and which are not, it is advisable to observe which essential oils are available for sale and at what price. Roughly, you can assume that all the better suited oils are relatively uncomplicated to distill from plants that are easy to obtain. Likewise, you can imagine why a single milliliter of rose oil can be compared to its weight in gold. We should not set the bar too high for hobby distilling of real essential oils. Distilling essential oils is possible with a 0.5 liter mini still, but in most cases not very productive.

You can distill almost anything—but not everything yields oil.

It is interesting to know that we get most essential oils in a better quality if we only perfuse the plant material with vapor and do not put it in the boiler first and boil it.

TIP | **Steam distillation**

I usually recommend using a still with as large a vapor chamber as possible to make hydrosols and essential oils, and to fill the chamber with the largest possible quantity of herbs to be distilled. It is only logical: The more oil-containing material we introduce, the more essential oils we can distill out. We already know half of the art. Simply try to fill your vapor chamber with as much plant material as possible.

Experimenting with rose petals in a thirty-liter still.

At the same time, you should be aware of the narrow openings from the head to the swan neck. If possible, place a fine copper sieve in front of the swan neck so that none of the plant material can get in and plug it up. In the worst case pressure could build up, forcing the head off the boiler. The escaping vapors may cause burns. Please always be aware of the danger!

Practical Distillation of Essential Oils

Distilling Cloves

To achieve initial success, I recommend you first make a test using cloves. It is easy to get large amounts of cloves and they are relatively inexpensive. At the same time, cloves contain a lot of oil and give off an intensely fragrant, clearly recognizable, and easily visible essential oil. It should also be possible for you to distill at least a few drops of essential oil with the smallest still.

Cloves: very fruitful and easy to distill!

In the photo you see how much you can get. The great thing about cloves is that we can see the oil clearly, because it stands out from the distillate by its color. Moreover, it is not absolutely necessary to crush the cloves beforehand or to distill them by steam. That would increase the quality and quantity, but this would be hard to measure without real laboratory equipment. You will see that cloves are just the right material for a first attempt.

Just put a handful of cloves into the boiler, or if available, into the vapor chamber of your still. Then fill the kettle to three-quarters with water and set it at a high heat. In contrast to alcohol, it is an advantage when distilling essential oils to heat the boiler rapidly so that you do not

Here I distilled an impressive amount of clove oil with a 0.5-liter column still.

Clove oil sinks to the bottom.

"over cook" the finer aromas and essential oils with a heat that increases slowly. When you are able to work more by routine later, I would advise when doing steam distillation to heat the boiler when it is open and only first set the column filled with the plants and the head on top when the water in the kettle is already boiling. This is something of a risk, but if you know your still and can trust yourself to do this step quickly, you can actually distill extremely high-quality essential oils rapidly.

With our cloves, when the water boils, pay attention to condensing it well! This is the second half of the art! We now know that yield is significantly increased if you use an efficient condensation method when distilling essential oils. At the beginning of the book we saw different designs. When distilling essential oils, a tightly fastened cooling circuit is in fact recommended, which always keeps pumping cold ice water from a bowl or sink through your still's condenser. The quantity and quality of the treasures you extract will reward you for this.

Set some glasses ready by the condenser that you can use to collect the distillate when it drips out. Depending on your still's purifying capacity, the first drops may still have a different odor or a different color, but after a short time the hydrosol should flow out cooled and quickly fill the first small bottles.

NOTE	Let the hydrosol rest

Just leave your distillate in peace!

Can you see the oil already? No? Leave the small bottles there for a day. Essential oil often remains finely distributed through the hydrosol and first has to "find" itself. Sufficient quantities of the tiny droplets of clove oil will soon collect on the bottom and combine with each other to form a small, easily visible oil bubble.

Clove oil is heavier than water, and it sinks downward. You can use a fine pipette to carefully "broach" the oil bubble and suck up the oil. What remains is the glass jar containing the hydrosol, which is best kept in the refrigerator for later use. Out of 300 ml of water with eighty grams of cloves you can readily distill 150 ml of a very intense hydrosol and several milliliters of essential oil. Smell the hydrosol carefully. You will notice how intensely the cloves come through and can certainly imagine how "forceful" and effective the hydrosols can also be. Here we can certainly perceive several valuable substances. Taste it carefully and feel the full disinfecting power of the cloves. The hydrosol—the little sister of the essential oil—does not have to hide.

IMPORTANT   Observe the effect

Be warned, the effect of fresh clove oil can be highly anesthetic, or even irritate the skin. Keep your distillate away from children. These experiences are another reason why I recommend you first distill clove oil. You can directly feel how the hydrosol has a strong antibacterial effect and immediately understand why we must be very careful handling plant distillates. They are not harmless, nor benign! Through distillation you will obtain highly effective plant substances which, depending on the contents and active ingredients of the plant, also require responsible handling, and as far as possible, some knowledge of the individual contents or effects. It is best to get a large book on herbs, or even a special book on aromatherapy, or the individual essential oils and hydrosols so you are well prepared to take on plants that have the biggest effects.

Attention, danger! Do not underestimate the efficacy of essential oils!

Distilling Lavender

For the next step, I would recommend distilling lavender. Lavender also has a relatively high oil content, and you should be able to extract at least one milliliter of essential oil and a fine hydrosol when using a 0.5-liter still, and if you cool it more intensely and use a large infusion basket, probably even more. While it does not matter with cloves, with lavender, you should definitely distill by steam—ideally, first set the filled column on the boiler only when the water in the kettle is already close to boiling. As soon as the steam penetrates the vapor chamber of your still and releases the fine essential oils from the lavender flowers a lovely lavender fragrance will spread all around you. Enjoy this pleasant side effect of your hobby; it usually smells good anywhere you are distilling. After the distillation, let the collected hydrosol rest a bit until the essential oils it contains combine with one another, and for lavender, float upward relatively easily and are readily visible, with a delicate, slightly yellowish honey hue.

Lavender—a friend to us all.

A good setup for distilling essential oils.

A glass flask also works well for collecting the distillate.

The "convenient plants" for distilling.

After these first two distillations, you are well equipped to take on all the other plants. You have learned that some oils dive to the bottom while others float on top. The color differences are also clear: clove oil is dark, while lavender oil shimmers, more bright and golden. Remember, some oils are crystal clear and are hard to recognize on the surface of the hydrosol, even if they are supposedly present there in larger quantities.

> **TIP** Plants you should try
>
> To have success in distilling your own essential oils, try using the following plants, all of which have a rather good oil content and are relatively easy to distill: Anise, star anise, fennel, caraway, mint, tarragon, marjoram, rosemary, juniper, nutmeg, ginger, eucalyptus, allspice, or calamus.
>
> You may also try using peels of citrus fruit, such as oranges or lemons, although these oils are usually pressed out cold. I wish you lots of fun and success with all these distillations.

What Is the Best Way for Me to Distill What?

In the early morning hours, shortly after sunrise, the concentration of essential oils is usually highest. Ideally, harvest fresh plant materials and distill them a short time later, when the plants have only slightly faded. In some plants, the oil-containing cells break up only after a prolonged drying time. The essential oils can then be distilled out much more easily. Lavender should always be dried for at least one and preferably two weeks before distilling it. Mint also tolerates a longer drying time very well. Since essential oils are fluid, any excessively long storage time can drastically reduce the amount of essential oils the plants contain. Most spices preserve their precious oils safely inside and can therefore also be distilled very well when dry. Cloves, fennel, anise, caraway, and juniper are among the most convenient plants that you can take from the kitchen rack as needed and distill successfully. For hobby distilling, it is worth it to keep a collection of dried materials on hand so that you always have enough oily bases for your own distillations.

For the very small quantities that we can distill privately, I recommend using the finest parts of the plant. For example, you should take the trouble to remove the lavender blossoms from the branch to get a higher yield. When distilling larger amounts you can distill the whole plant, including the woody parts. You can prepare other plants with leaves or needles by chopping them finely with a knife or scissors. Coarse or harder spices, such as cloves or juniper, should be crushed a bit with a food processor, so that when they are opened up and broken the way is free for the vapor to penetrate inside, giving you a more intense and higher yield.

Hydrosols

One thing we have already learned from cloves: hydrosols do not have to hide! Even if you cannot extract any essential oils from a large amount of plant material, simply because many plants do not have them available in sufficient quantities and the legal boundaries limit us too much, there is always enough to make a good herbal distillate. Hydrosols are child's play to extract and very effective. It is worth putting together a small collection of the most important plants for the most important domestic uses and turning them into hydrosols in good time.

Higher yield through more preparation.

Freshly distilled hydrosols can be kept refrigerated for months, sometimes even for years, and used as required. You surely have a small compartment in your refrigerator free for your self-distilled home drug store or for secret spice enhancers.

Lavender from a sachet bag.

Which Plants for What Purpose?

Anise

Anise is a well-known and popular specialty, especially for distilling schnapps, which we already have some experience with from making spirits. As a healing plant, anise has an antiseptic effect, it promotes digestion and relieves cramps, and is a mucus expectorant, which is why it can be found in a whole range of medicinal preparations, including delicious anise cough drops, but also teas and all sorts of delicious dishes. In higher doses, anise not only has a soothing effect, but can even have an anesthetic effect. In India, people chew anise as a kind of dessert, which freshens the breath, improves digestion, and soothes the body.

Anise: high oil content and many uses.

Making essential oils from anise is relatively easy, since anise has a high oil content, and we can therefore easily obtain measurable results even with a 0.5-liter still. The ideal way to extract anise oil is by passing water vapor through anise seeds. We use a still that is also suitable for water vapor distillation—for example, a column still—and fill the vapor chamber with the maximum possible amount of anise, which could even be 200 g. The optimal method would be to crush the seeds slightly in a mortar or a food processor. Just running the processor briefly should be enough; the seeds should only be slightly crushed and not pulverized. Fill the still boiler with about 300 ml of water. At the end of the distillation, we should have collected 200 ml of anise water with a yellowish, floating layer of pure anise oil. Depending on the amount of anise seeds used, we can extract one to two grams of essential oils using a mini still and collect it in a narrow jar using a pipette. This oil forms an ideal base for an admixture and use as a base for liqueurs, sweets, cooking recipes, and healing remedies. Anise water is a blessing for coughs and you can gargle with it for a scratchy throat.

Apples

The apple is one of the most popular and versatile plants for us do-it-yourselfers, mainly because they can be harvested in abundant quantities without any great effort and further processed. With a little technology, little effort is involved in pressing juice and cider, and the yield is mostly very tasty. Unfortunately, apple aromas are not very distinctive, and an apple distillate rarely tastes very strongly of apples, so apple brandies (with the exception of aged Calvados) play a rather minor role.

The apple is the hobby distillers' best friend!

For us hobby distillers, apples are available year-round, are uniquely convenient, and are an easy-to-process base that we should not neglect, even if we later only distill out the pure alcohol. It quickly becomes well worth it to see the apple as a friend and use it accordingly, especially for hobby distilling. From only thirty-three pounds (15 kg) of apples we can extract ten liters of juice, which we can ferment into apple wine and distill into two liters of apple schnapps.

Basil

This herb is often underestimated, although we almost all love its flavor in Italian or Thai cuisine. In upscale bars, we can discover some delicious cocktails with fresh basil, and as an essential oil, basil provides great aromatherapy. As a fragrance, basil is soothing, an antidepressant, and lightens the mood, and is also successfully used in medicine for coughs or headaches, as well as for digestive problems and inflammations.

Basil is uniquely delicious and often underestimated.

Basil essential oil is easy to distill by steam, at least theoretically, but the quantities you can expect would be too small to let you work successfully using a 0.5-liter still. For 1 ml of basil oil, we would have to distill at least 500 g of plant material. To do this, you should use at least a two-liter still. Fortunately, basil hydrosol is also enriched with valuable ingredients and has many good uses, even if it has a rather fresh and green fragrance in contrast to the oil, or the basil plant itself.

For the hydrosol, distill 70 g of freshly cut leaves with 300 ml of water and break the distillation off as late as possible after you have extracted one hundred millileters; this is how you obtain an excellent and highly aromatic basil hydrosol. To generally enhance your well-being (or for digestive problems), drink a cup of it every morning. On a stressful day, you can breathe in the pure essential oil deeply to immediately feel an invigorating and refreshing effect. Basil hydrosol also has an invigorating effect when you moisten a compress with it and apply it to your forearms for ten minutes.

Pears

The pear is my personal favorite fruit, presumably because I have unique childhood memories of hours climbing up Grandma's pear tree, and the smell of Williams pears can still elicit a smile. Today, above all, when it originates from a fine liquor. But all the other pear varieties are also very good for mashing and distilling.

Wash pears before making a mash.

Savory

Savory is an herb that we neglect in our kitchens, but it is highly aromatic and can be used to complement thyme, oregano, and most other Mediterranean herbs. Hardly anyone knows that it also has an antibacterial effect and helps to alleviate stomach pain because of its anti-convulsive effect. One more reason to include it in the list of distilling herbs, even though we probably cannot distill out any essential oils from this herb using a tabletop still.

To make a harmonious hydrosol, distill 70 g of the fine flower tips with 300 ml of water and end the distillation when you have collected about 80 ml of the hydrosol.

Gentian

We can distill a fine specialty from gentian, which is underestimated in many places. To do this, a mash is made of gentian—actually from gentian root—and it is fermented and distilled like a pure-bred fine brandy. In view of the many steps required to harvest and process the root, which are protected under nature conservancy, it is a miracle that you can drink a "gentian" liqueur at so reasonable a price. Likely this is due to the distinctive, rather bitter aroma, which is certainly not for everyone.

Processing gentian yourself is probably not a good idea, but you can easily buy a few hundred grams of dried gentian root from an herbal supplier and use them to fortify your own schnapps or liqueur. Certainly gentian would be a fine addition in your own grain mash.

Gentian: the delicious classic from the mountains.

Strawberries

Strawberries do not distill well, but I mention them here to briefly explain making flavorings with strawberries. If you read that a product contains natural flavors, that does not mean that those flavorings were made from strawberries. There are more strawberry flavorings worldwide than there are strawberries. Most strawberry flavorings are not made from these small fruits, and unfortunately, the manufacturers do not reveal from which base the strawberry flavors were extracted; at the same time they deny that they are made from sawdust, wood, or potatoes. Nevertheless, the industry may offer natural strawberry flavors even if they are not made from strawberries.

Strawberries are difficult to work with.

When you look around, you will discover thousands of strawberry products, such as toothpaste, chewing gum, yogurt, jam—everything is possible—but there are hardly any liquors. This is because mashing and fermenting transforms the aroma of the fresh strawberries into a rather unpleasant, mushy green scent. It is also difficult to capture the fine strawberry aromas when making a *Geist*. What works well with raspberries we can try with wild strawberries, but when you are distilling it seems that the right aroma does not want to enter into the *Geist*. At least not in my attempts . . .

Eucalyptus

Very helpful plant— unfortunately hard for us to obtain.

This plant is generally well-known for its camphor-like fragrances and accompanying effects, which are especially beneficial for breathing. This is why eucalyptus is an ideal ingredient in oral rinses for most respiratory illnesses or colds and in bath oil or in cough drops. You could almost describe eucalyptus as a miraculous general remedy, so versatile are its effects. Eucalyptus is one of the plants with the strongest antiseptic effect. It also works to lower fevers, it relieves cramps, is a mucus expectorant, and is invigorating. This creates a wide range of possible applications, from the kitchen, to medicine and perfumery.

> **IMPORTANT** Caution!
>
> Larger amounts act on the nerve center. Eucalyptus should therefore not be inhaled by children.

Eucalyptus leaves should be harvested as fresh as possible, carefully dried, and processed chopped or in broken pieces, which is likely only rarely possible. If you discover some eucalyptus trees during a holiday, do not be afraid to pick up the fresh leaves, dry them in the sun, and take them home with you to distill. Do not transport fresh eucalyptus in a bag, because due to the moisture it usually tends to become moldy. For drying, the leaves should be layered loosely and with plenty of air.

Eucalyptus has a relatively high oil content. Depending on the quality, you can count on obtaining one to two grams of essential oil per 100 g of leaves. That is an amount that is definitely possible to see. But eucalyptus can do even more, because even the hydrosol has an antibacterial effect, and therefore works really well for cleaning sick rooms or baths. To obtain 100 ml of a perfect hydrosol, distill 100 g freshly cut eucalyptus leaves with 300 ml of water directly in the kettle.

Fennel

Fennel is very similar to anise and is often used together with anise in various liqueurs and schnapps, but also in natural remedies. Medically, fennel has antibacterial, detoxifying, appetizing, diuretic, and anti-flatulence effects, and also works well as a seasoning for cooking. Fennel is good for distilling, because you can buy it dried all year round as a spice and then distill it.

Do you like fennel? Then you will certainly like to distill it.

The same basic principles apply for distilling fennel as for anise. Fennel is usually extracted by steam distillation. For a bigger yield, the seeds should be slightly moistened or crushed briefly in a food processor. Fennel produces relatively abundant results. You can distill up to two grams of oil per 100 g and thus obtain a delicious hydrosol. A good mixing ratio is 200 g of fennel to 300 ml of water if you do not distill by steam, and this amount will fit into your still boiler without boiling over.

You can make generous use of the hydrosol in the kitchen as a seasoning for baking bread, as well as in soups, sauces, or stews. Cosmetically, fennel water also has an astringent effect, and therefore works to tighten the skin; it can be applied to tired eyelids, and thanks to its antiseptic effect it is also ideal for wiping inflamed eyes.

Spruce Needles

Spruce needles are widely known for soothing and relaxing baths, or for inhalations for colds and coughs. The hydrosol and essential oil, which smell pleasantly of the forest, can be used in many ways, both internally and externally, and have a positive effect on the respiratory tract and on the joints in the case of rheumatism or gout, as well as on our well-being. If we take a closer look, for example, in Austria, we also find spruce needle liqueurs and schnapps. You see that it quickly becomes worthwhile to bring a couple spruce branches back with you from a walk in the forest and experiment with them. It is hard to do anything wrong; spruce grows abundantly in many latitudes and the needles are easy to harvest and process—best by steam distillation of the dried, chopped needles.

A home country miracle—easy to find and to distill.

Here I am cutting up spruce needles in my kitchen . . .

Ginger

My personal favorite spice: ginger.

Ginger is my favorite spice for a number of reasons, but mainly because I really love its intense aroma in food and tea. Thanks to its mucus expectorant, disinfecting, and anti-inflammatory properties, I also appreciate ginger on cold days, when I prepare some fresh tea of grated ginger, which I let boil for a few minutes and then, before I serve it, add a pinch of pepper, a lot of lemon, and some honey to taste.

Ginger has an advantage for distilling, because it also distills very well when it is dried. Ginger then yields relatively good results, and we should be able to distill up to two milliliters very fine ginger oil from 50 g finely cut ginger. The hydrosol makes a good tonic for dabbing the skin if you are feeling stressed, unsettled, or annoyed. Ginger helps you find new courage and inner balance. Ginger stimulates the mind and strengthens the body. Alternatively, you can also add the hydrosols to a fragrance lamp, perhaps with the addition of a few drops of citrus oil for clarifying, and avail yourself of the creativity-fostering room fragrance.

Raspberries

These berries are a real joy in the garden, and not just for delicious compotes and jams. Raspberries, with their fine aroma—which transfers very well to a liquor—provide us a lot of fun, especially for distilling alcohol. Try it out. Raspberries are easy to get and just as easy to transform into a fine *Geist*. The raspberry offers more, because you can also cut the leaves up finely and use them dried as a substitute for black tea. Thanks to the anti-convulsive effect, raspberry leaves are also very popular with midwives for obstetrics. Raspberry blossom oils are unfortunately impossible to distill, but they are used in the perfume industry because of the fine pleasant fragrance.

Delicious and easy to gather.

Chamomile

We all know chamomile as chamomile tea, which we like to drink for stomachaches. But chamomile also has an enormous anti-inflammatory effect.

. . . and here I am macerating a jar of fresh raspberries in vodka.

There are several chamomile species, and these differ greatly in what they contain and their mode of action. The so-called German chamomile produces a rather viscous, blue essential oil that is only rarely possible for us hobby distillers to extract, just like most other flower oils. Extracting the oils of Roman chamomile also requires considerably larger amounts of plant material than we could distill in our small tabletop stills. We must therefore confine ourselves to their hydrosols, which we can use primarily as a soothing facial lotion when combined with other flower hydrosols, such as rose or violet. For medical applications, such as for cleaning wounds, it is usually better to use a freshly brewed and long-steeped tea or a macerate (a cold water extract) than the hydrosol.

Caraway

My recommendation: Distill a caraway *Geist*. You will be inspired!

A drink made of caraway is a specialty that is particularly popular in Germany; you can make it just like an "Anis," and it can help with digestion problems. For us hobby distillers, caraway schnapps is made as a *Geist*, because we distill out the aromas with alcohol. According to EU regulations, caraway digestif (*Kümmel*) is a liquor, which can only be called *Kümmel* as long as it does not contain anything except caraway (and dill) and the caraway flavor dominates. Just try it out; it is relatively simple to macerate caraway seeds in a neutral grain spirit or vodka and distill a fine *Kümmel*.

Caraway hydrosol in a 0.5-liter column still.

It is just as easy to extract essential oils and intense hydrosols from caraway. Caraway has relatively high oil content, and depending on the quality, you should be able to produce useful quantities of essential oils even with a legal tabletop still. You can reckon to get about one to two milliliters of essential oils from each 40 g of caraway; do not overfill your still, since the seeds swell up during distillation. Caraway hydrosol works very well as a seasoning, and like *Kümmelschnaps*, stimulates digestion and gives you a good appetite.

Lavender

Lavender is the friend of all distillers. A plant we love that can be distilled very well thanks to its relatively high concentration of essential oils. To make essential oils and hydrosols, it is best to use the herb chopped small and dried and distill it by water vapor in your still's infusion basket. You will surely get an intense hydrosol, and depending on your still's possibilities, also with a few drops of bright, possibly slightly yellowish essential oils floating on top. For a well-balanced hydrosol, distill just the first 50 ml of a mixture of 50 g of lavender blossoms with 300 ml of water directly in the boiler.

Lavender is best distilled using water vapor.

Lavender has an antibacterial and anti-inflammatory effect, but it is also stimulating and calming at the same time and enhances self-confidence. The hydrosol is a good additive to cleaning solutions, but also works well in all kinds of cosmetic applications, in pure form as a treat for your skin, or it can be added to bath water. Lavender has almost no role in cooking or for making alcohol, although it is used as a fine additive for some kinds of gin or herbal schnapps and in a few liqueurs.

Linden Blossoms

It is easy to find these flowers in the northern hemisphere, and their healing effect has been known since ancient times. Linden flowers have a soothing, relaxing, diuretic, and anti-inflammatory effect. Before you harvest them, make sure that the tree's owner agrees to let you pluck his flowers. You need 50 g of these with 300 ml of water to save the first 50 ml of the distillation as a fine hydrosol. Linden flower hydrosol, combined with rose and chamomile hydrosols, works perfectly, especially as a gentle skin lotion with soothing effects, but also as a gentle massage medium for tense muscles.

My tip: homemade skin lotion from linden flowers.

Laurel

Does laurel grow in your garden as a little tree? Then you are lucky, and can harvest a few of the leaves fresh and distill them. Just 50 ml of the finely cut, fresh (or dried) leaves with 300 ml of water are enough to obtain 50 ml of an excellent hydrosol. If you want to distill essential oils, try using a maximum amount of leaves and distill using water vapor. Laurel is very versatile, and despite its high antiseptic effect, is very kind to the skin. Besides this, it has a vitalizing effect, as well as promoting digestion and blood circulation, and enhances self-confidence.

In the kitchen, laurel is well-known as a seasoning for all kinds of food. You can also use your home-distilled hydrosol for seasoning and "spicing up" your dishes later. Add laurel hydrosol or oil to a fragrance lamp and the scent will drive away most of the insects flying around. Alternatively, you can apply the hydrosol directly to your skin with a soft cloth or sponge and drive away insects around you and do your skin good at the same time.

Marjoram

Marjoram: not only for cooking.

Marjoram is also a very much underestimated herb with a wide range of uses and effects in the kitchen, as well as in the medical field and in natural cosmetics. Marjoram is exhilarating, relaxing, and easing, and at the same time stimulates blood circulation and relieves pain. To make an intense and healing marjoram hydrosol, distill 80 g of marjoram with 300 ml of water. Distill as long as necessary until you have obtained 80 ml, then break off the distillation. With some luck, there will one or so droplets of essential marjoram oil floating on top that you can just leave there. Use the fresh hydrosol as a base to lighten your morning mood in case of winter depression, along with one or two drops of bergamot and lavender in the fragrance lamp. The hydrosol can also be used as an additional seasoning for cooking.

Lemon Balm

A fine oil with tradition.

Lemon balm is often underappreciated, although it is a pleasant and versatile, friendly plant with many uses. It is difficult to produce essential oils from fresh lemon balm, since the herb unfortunately does not contain much oil. Perhaps you will discover one drop or two floating on your

Distilling lemon balm in the Aroma Museum.

hydrosol. The hydrosol is particularly versatile, and is distinguished by its known calming and skin soothing properties. For distillation, use freshly harvested leaves. Try it using 50 g of cut leaves with 300 ml of water and distill 50 to 100 ml of an intense, pleasantly fragrant lemon balm hydrosol.

Mint

Due to its health-promoting aroma, mint or peppermint is very popular as a tea, for inhaling, and also in cough drops or medicines (Japanese healing oil). At the same time, we also know mint in all sorts of sweets and refreshing summer drinks. Its main ingredient, menthol, has a beneficial effect on sniffles and colds, and can also be distilled in small amounts to make a hydrosol. Large quantities of essential oils are contained in fresh and dried peppermint. Due to the large volume of plant pieces necessary, it can still be difficult to distill the oils in a mini still. I recommend you distill 60 g of crushed leaves with 300 ml of water to make about 60 ml of a refreshing hydrosol. Sample the difference between steam distillation and a conventional distillation with the leaves in the boiler.

Mint: intense effect also as a remedy.

Cloves

Cloves are an aromatic feature and a strong flavor carrier, and not just in Christmas baked goods, but in all kinds of liqueurs and schnapps. Cloves are one of the oil-richest spices and therefore easy to distill. The best way to do this is by steam distillation with a suitable still. You can see clearly (see below) what quantities you can produce with a small still. You might try your first experiments with clove oil, because this is not only easy to make, but can also be especially good for using in further ways.

IMPORTANT	Attention!

Cloves yield a very intense essential oil when distilled and an almost equally intense hydrosol, which has a strong antiseptic effect and must be used very sparingly in its pure form. You should keep clove oil away from children, do not put it in your eyes or on your mucous membranes, and only take diluted clove oil internally.

Fifty grams of cloves yields 100 ml of hydrosol or 2 ml of clove oil.

Fine clove oil from a mini still.

It is a powerful antibacterial miracle agent for external use and can be used, like its less intense hydrosol, to heal wounds, and as a disinfectant for all skin diseases. Clove oil helps a good deal for toothaches, because it has the power to numb the spot where it is dabbed with a cotton swab within seconds. Besides this, the hydrosol is also very versatile, for example, as a disinfectant or mouthwash. You can also use clove herbal essence in the kitchen to aromatize herbs and sauces, or to make gingerbread. And if you want another tip, add the oil with a little orange oil to a fragrance lamp and a wonderful Christmas scent quickly emerges in your surroundings.

NOTE	Separate the oil

During distillation, clove oil settles downward, since, unlike most other essential oils, it is heavier than the watery hydrosol. We can use a fine pipette to conveniently remove it from the bottom of a reagent glass after it has rested briefly and separate it from the milky, cloudy hydrosol.

Orange oil is relatively easy to extract.

Oranges

In oranges, the essential oils sit directly in the fine pores of the outer orange peel and are usually cold-pressed. One of the reasons why essential orange oils, like other citrus oils, are often less expensive to buy and are used as a "cheap" base for all kinds of fragrance mixtures. Oranges are easy to get in relatively large quantities, and the oil is even easier to extract. You can use a zester or a good knife to try to cut the outer orange peel into fine strips to distill it. You have a good chance of even extracting a few drops of the essential oil through distillation.

We use much more of the orange, primarily the delicious juice, which we drink pure, or as a base for all kinds of liqueurs. In my Spanish times, I enriched the freshly squeezed juice with sugar and fermented it with baker's yeast to obtain fresh light orange wines. The dried peels give us an important bitter taste and other flavors that are also an important ingredient in making liqueurs, as well as in Christmas baked goods.

Oranges as a miracle fruit?

I would almost like to call oranges a versatile miracle fruit and suggest using them to every distiller if they grew in our own gardens. Thus, we are limited to buying relatively expensive oranges in the supermarket, which unfortunately significantly reduces our opportunities to experiment freely. Take care that you purchase untreated oranges, if possible organic quality if you process the peel, because who knows what has been sprayed on them.

Orange oils irritate the skin and should therefore only be used sparingly. In addition, they have an invigorating, appetizing effect and enhance physical defenses. It is not only the large amounts of vitamin C in the juice that gives oranges their effect, but also the fragrance alone does a lot to enhance self-confidence and provide new energy.

There is also fine essential oil from orange blossoms that is not something hobby distillers can manufacture. In the industry it is extracted, like many other flower oils, using the solvent hexane.

Roses

Naturally, we cannot leave roses out, especially because rose oil is a fine treasure—something we quickly realize when we try to distill it. It will not be possible for us to extract a single drop in hobby distilling, just like other delicate flower oils. To do this, we would need much larger amounts of fresh petals than we could put in our tabletop stills.

For a fantastically intense rose water, distill the first 50 ml of a mixture of 300 ml of water with 50 g of freshly harvested rose petals directly in the boiler. You get a fine, skin-soothing facial lotion that can also be mixed with sage or thyme hydrosol to make a mouthwash. Rose water has an antiviral and antiseptic effect. You can also use rose water in the kitchen, and you will surely quickly discover delicious recipes using rose water if you just start looking for them.

The noble queen among fragrant plants.

Hobby still "Italia" in a rose garden.

Rosemary

Fruitful and versatile rosemary.

This plant, like thyme or lavender, contains relatively abundant oil, and it should be possible for you to extract ten to twenty drops of highly fragrant rosemary oil without any problem, even from a small amount of hydrosol, such as 100 ml made from 80 g of fresh chopped rosemary leaves with 300 ml of water. Rosemary has a beneficial effect on blood circulation, inhibits inflammation, is a mucus expectorant, and is antispasmodic, and therefore also works very well in all kinds of mixtures, especially for the relief of coughs and colds. In high doses rosemary oil can cause skin irritation, which is why the essential oils are best applied only as mixtures with lavender or other oils. You can use the hydrosol directly as a hair lotion or as a refreshing and cleansing facial lotion for bad skin.

Rosemary is an indispensable ingredient in the kitchen, so it is only logical that you can also use the hydrosol to season all sorts of soups, sauces, or other dishes. And if you want to internalize knowledge about all the possible kinds of herbal schnapps quickly, you will soon realize that rosemary often plays an important role in them. By the way, I steam two drops of rosemary oil with some mint oil and thyme in the fragrance lamp on my desk. Even after a long working day, this re-stimulates the gray cells and increases concentration.

Sage

Sage has been an additive in cough drops and in all sorts of teas and soothing mixtures for coughs and colds for a long time. No wonder, because sage not only tastes good, it is also highly antibacterial and a

Freshly harvested sage just before it is distilled.

fungicide. Sage oil is also relatively easy to distill. Even in small quantities, it should be possible for you to extract one to two milliliters of genuine essential sage oils by steam distillation without any serious complications. And if not? Do not worry, the hydrosol is also highly effective and can be applied with great effect as a gargle solution for throat inflammation. It also serves as a base for cosmetics, such as shaving lotion, facial or hair lotion, and as a deodorant.

IMPORTANT	Caution!

Please always proceed carefully with your distillates. Sage may appear to be more harmless than it is because it is frequently used in teas and delicious cough drops. But sage contains the neurotoxin thujone, which can not only cause hallucinations and confusion, but also permanently damage your nerves and lead to epilepsy. Thujone was formerly an important ingredient in the cult drink Absinthe, and now only tiny quantities are permitted in this drink. Sage oil can contain up to sixty percent thujone! In countries such as France and Great Britain, the sale of sage oil is therefore prohibited, or only allowed for medical purposes through pharmacies. Please keep this knowledge in mind and always proceed carefully with your distillates. Essential oils are highly effective, concentrated plant substances and should not be underestimated.

Important to know: Sage can cause hallucinations and damage your nerves.

Chives

This is a widely popular spicy herb, and we can hardly imagine our kitchens without it. Chives not only contribute to delicious dishes, but also medically act as a healing plant for lack of appetite, flatulence, coughs, springtime lethargy, hypertension, and stomach inflammation. Due to its broad range of effects, chives work well for mixing into medicinal liqueurs and herbal schnapps, but you should take care with the dosage so that its dominant, sharp onion flavor does not become too strong.

Thyme

Thyme is one of the herbs that I can very well tolerate, and I have intense recollections of its fragrance. Thyme reminds me of my early years in the hot mountain valleys of Andalusia, where an intense thyme fragrance pervaded the entire environment. At that time, I did not yet know how well you can distill thyme. We just seasoned our homemade cheese and other food with it. Spanish thyme is much milder than the "normal" herb because it lacks the substance thymol, but it is just as good to use. Its effects are relatively well-known, so thyme is mostly used in mucus expectorant mixtures for coughs and colds—including for children—and for inhalation. At the same time, thyme also has a pain-relieving, skin-friendly soothing effect.

If you distill 150 g of the freshly rubbed-off leaves with 300 g of water, you are sure to get 150 ml of a very high-quality thyme distillate that you can use immediately. It is very likely that there will be a few drops of essential oil floating on top, because thyme has a relatively high oil content. If you are targeting essential oils, it should be possible to use a 0.5-liter still to obtain a useful amount. Try it out. Dried thyme can also be distilled, but the leaves lose a lot of essential oil during storage time which you then notice from the low yield.

Vanilla

Vanilla: Well-loved fragrance that we better not distill ourselves.

We know vanilla well from its scent, and most of us have loved it from childhood. The vanilla aroma appears to be extremely sweetly fragrant, and is used for all kinds of cosmetic, medical, and culinary applications. The only problem that keeps us from "making it ourselves" is the relatively high purchase price for "fresh" vanilla pods. The essential oil of the pods, which unfortunately give a poor yield, is very difficult to distill out, which is why commercially available essential vanilla oil is usually washed out with alcohol. Strictly speaking, purchased vanilla oils are therefore not essential oils, but alcohol solutions that contain up to twenty-four different aromas from vanilla pods. They are nevertheless delicious.

Because vanilla is difficult to distill, I recommend using it as an ingredient in a maceration (vanilla vodka), or to refine an over-distilled liquor (gin). If you decide you can afford it, you can also make a fine vanilla water that requires considerably larger quantities of vanilla than if you use the pods only as an additive or for seasoning. Use vanilla water anywhere you might otherwise use rose water in the kitchen. Vanilla encourages appetite and buying, and also fosters a harmonious mood, is an aphrodisiac, and enhances concentration.

Violets

These small plants grow at the edge of every forest in northern latitudes and are therefore very easy to harvest in spring when they flower. For 50 ml of a fine, fresh violet hydrosol, it is enough to add 50 g of the fresh flowers to 300 ml of water and distill. Unfortunately, it is hard for us hobby distillers to extract the very fine violet fragrance or its essential oils. Fresh violets work very well for experimenting to see whether you can't extract some of the fragrance with alcohol, water, or fat after oil. In the industry, violets are extracted using the solvent hexane, which is not recommended for private use. You can certainly use the hydrosol safely as a facial lotion, and also in a fine fifty-percent mixture with chamomile or rose hydrosol, all of which are very well tolerated by the skin and have a toning effect. With purchased violet extracts and oils I would be rather more reserved because of the chemicals.

Violets as a hydrosol.

Juniper

Juniper is easy to come by in the northern hemisphere, and for this reason alone is already precious for us hobby distillers. Keep a look out on your next walk; juniper trees are often cultivated as hedges between the grounds in modern housing developments. Juniper is uniquely versatile. Even the wood of some varieties of juniper continue to emit fragrance for many years, and cut into pieces, it can be beautifully decorative in a room. Juniper is a true friend, because we can use it to spice up our food, make all sorts of fine drinks, and in versatile ways for medical and cosmetic purposes. Depending on the variety, we can produce essential oils in smaller quantities, as well as fine hydrosols using only the crushed berries. Juniper oil has a strengthening and constructive effect, and has a strong, cleansing effect on the soul and the skin, which is why juniper distillates are often used in skin creams. But beware: In large quantities, pure juniper oil can also act as a skin irritant. In contrast, the hydrosol can be used as a disinfecting facial lotion. For a good hydrosol, crush 125 g of juniper berries and pour 200 ml of water over them. After a short rest period, distill out 100 ml of the finest juniper water for various applications before breaking off the distillation.

Juniper: the distiller's favorite plant.

Cinnamon

Cinnamon, like vanilla, is a very well-known and loved aroma in the kitchen, and is clearly recognizable. Outside the kitchen it is mostly used in combination with other fragrances and flavors. Cinnamon offers strong anti-inflammatory, antibacterial properties, and should also be used with caution. Direct application to the skin can lead to severe skin irritation; as a fragrance or remedy a few individual drops suffice, and these are best mixed with a carrier oil or other essential oils. Unfortunately, cinnamon is not as fruitful in distillation as we would like it to be. With a mini still, it would be difficult to produce essential cinnamon oils in a usable quantity. As with cloves, the essential oil sinks downward. You can distill the entire plant, but most likely you will fall back on using the bark of the cinnamon tree. The hydrosol works well as a base in a fragrance lamp. Especially during the Christmas season, you can create a homey, warming ambiance with a few additional drops of orange or vanilla oil in your fragrance lamp.

All Kinds of
Different Recipes

Spaghetti with Basil-Thyme Sauce

Add two sardine fillets, two tablespoons of yogurt, fifteen basil leaves, the green leaves from three stems of thyme, one clove of garlic, 100 ml of basil herbal essence, and 100 ml of thyme herbal essence together in a food processor.

Stir this sauce directly over al dente hot pasta and serve immediately.

Lemon Balm-Rosemary Face Lotion

Distill 20 g of fresh lemon balm, 10 g of thyme, 10 g of rosemary, and 10 g of mint together with 300 ml of water. This hydrosol is an excellent skin lotion with a soothing and stimulating effect.

Mint-Sage Skin Lotion

You can easily distill a refreshing whole body skin lotion with a stimulating effect for tired legs by distilling 30 g mint together with 10 g each of sage and rosemary. If you add 300 ml of water, you can distill 50 ml for direct use. This also works very well using dried plant material.

> **TIP** | Another version
>
> For a skin lotion against oily skin, use violets instead of the refreshing mint.

Mouthwash for a Toothache

Mix three parts marjoram hydrosol with one part clove hydrosol and use it to rinse your teeth three times a day. For severe pain, use a cotton swab to dab the same mixture of oil on the painful spot on the tooth. In case of severe pain, increase the proportion of clove oil.

Mouthwash for Gargling Against Inflammation

Mix 40 ml chamomile hydrosol with 30 ml each of lavender and mint hydrosol to make an anti-inflammatory mouthwash for gargling in the morning.

Wash Lotions for Intimate Areas

Mix 50 ml of rose water with the same amount of sage hydrosol to make a delicate cleaning water for the intimate areas of your body.

Cough and Throat Teas

If you are really up to your neck in things, I recommend using a strong peppermint tea with a few drops of peppermint oil. If your still is too small to distill your own mint oil, just buy a bottle of Japanese medicinal oil, or even better, an organic peppermint oil. You will notice the liberating effect with every sip—and even more when inhaling the fresh mint vapors above the cup.

Anti-Stress Hydrosol

Mix equal parts basil and rosemary hydrosols for a strengthening miracle remedy; during stressful times take three teaspoonfuls slowly and deliberately immediately after waking up.

Nerve-Strengthening Herbal Distillate

Mix 40 ml of lemon balm hydrosol with 30 ml of mint and linden flower hydrosol each and take three teaspoonfuls each morning at breakfast.

Digestive Tonic

At lunch, enjoy a teaspoon of this effective tonic to resolve stomach and digestive problems within a few days. Mix 40 ml of anise hydrosol with 30 ml of fennel and 30 ml of sage hydrosol and store it in the refrigerator.

Inhalation Mixture for the Respiratory Tract

For an inhalation, pour equal parts steaming hot hydrosols of basil, mint, and sage into a bowl and breathe in the steam. Also suitable for children—and as a room fragrance in your fragrance lamp during cough and cold times.

Spruce Needle Bath Salts

Use spruce needles that are slightly dried and cut into pieces; put as many as possible in the vapor chamber of your still. Also fill the boiler about half full with spruce needles and then fill it up with water.

When you distill, you get a finely scented hydrosol with a little essential oil floating on top. Add a few drops of green food coloring so that it looks beautiful later. Depending on the amount of hydrosol you have available, dissolve as much fine salt as possible in it. You can dissolve about 35 g per 100 ml at room temperature. If possible, do not heat the hydrosol above 104°F to maintain the good aroma of the spruce needles. After the salt has dissolved, let the moisture slowly evaporate while you keep stirring it over several days. Whatever remains in the end is a dry green salt with the aroma of spruce needles.

Just before distilling the spruce needle hydrosol.

Rubbing Alcohol

To make your own rubbing alcohol, first distill a bottle of white wine.[26] You should get at least 100 ml of wine spirit with a content of 40% ABV before you end the distillation. Add twenty drops of spruce needle oil and sage oil, as well as forty drops of rosemary, pine, and mint oil. These are quantities that, with a little patience, you can distill in one day using steam distillation even in the miniature format, since the plants are all quite high yielding. Alternatively, you can also use purchased essential oil, in which case I would advise you use organic quality. The peppermint oil can also be replaced with 1 g purchased menthol crystals. It is also an exciting experience to try this with pure menthol.

Rubbing alcohol has an invigorating, cooling, and circulation promoting effect, and works very well for rubbing tired legs. In addition, rubbing alcohol relieves the symptoms of bruises, sprains, and muscle pain and strains, as well as poor blood circulation. If you add an onion and let the whole thing steep for fourteen days you get an excellent scalp and hair tonic.

TIP | **Write everything down!**

Even if it is difficult for you to do, you should write down all your experimental setups, volume ratios, and mixtures in a distiller's book. Only if you get accustomed to carefully documenting everything from the beginning can you research any deviations or special features later on and find out any errors you made.

Imagine if you discover an exceptionally delicious gin, a unique recipe of the century, but do not notice it until a year later, when you again sip something from that almost forgotten bottle. Could you now recall the composition and reconstruct the recipe? You will hardly believe it, but a lot of drinks have been created by chance, and sometimes it took decades until it was recognized why that drink was so particularly tasty.

---

[26] Paracelsus said that only wine spirits should be used for medical applications. I say he is right! Nowadays, it would be appropriate to use an organic wine if you really mean well.

Hydrosols in the refrigerator.

For example, wine was distilled to reduce the volume. This was the only way it was cost effectively possible to ship larger quantities overseas as commercial goods. There, the brandy was supposed to then be diluted with water back into wine and sold. The long storage in wooden barrels changed the flavor distinctly and a new specialty was born: brandy. The same is true of rum, and of course, Aquavit, which is said to be still transported all around the world today to let it age.

But back to the notes. Also label your bottles and distillates. At first it may still be easy to distinguish these by scent and recall the respective distillation. But I can promise you that you will soon have doubts when distinguishing among the individual distillates; at the same time, the solution is quite simple. Keep a diary, write down everything, and label and mark everything carefully. This way, you can always determine everything with certainty. Trust me, because I speak from experience. Otherwise, you will find things becoming like my refrigerator, where I wanted to keep various hydrosols as seasoning for cooking and thought I could save myself the bother of labeling because of the small bottles. An error . . .

Further Recommendations

I hope that I have communicated a little bit of the fun of distilling to you with this book. It was an important matter for me to be able to show how simple and straightforward distilling actually is. I hope I have succeeded. In the end, it is just about doing it. Distill whenever you feel like it. It always works, even by the way and in between. I have heated a still without a condenser just for fun, and steamed water with orange peel and cloves in the chamber. In the end, this is not any more complicated than putting a tea light under a fragrance lamp, even if the flame is slightly larger. With a little experience, you will soon be able to develop a good sense of what goes together, what is possible, what distillate from which distillation is worth keeping and storing—and what distillation you just let run for fun and interest. Doing it is ultimately what separates us from success. The difference between getting started, the beginning, taking action—which always comes down to a result—and in contrast to the rather retarding effect of "thinking it over again" or waiting. Just do it; you have nothing to lose. In the worst case, your distillate will not taste very good and you have lost a few dollars. What does it matter? You have learned something and are ready for the next attempt.

I would recommend to keep informed and stock up on supplies from the right places. Find herbal, yeast, fruit, and accessory suppliers that you trust. Especially if you want to use your distillates, it does not matter whether you make a fine liquor for drinking, an aromatic hydrosol for cooking, or a cosmetic or remedy for external application. Be careful to obtain high-quality and fine ingredients—organic if possible—because you should always treat yourself to the best. You only live once. Why save on yourself?

And it definitely makes sense and is recommended that you keep yourself informed. For some topics the internet is a great source. For example, if you want to know more about essential oils and their manufacture or applications.

> **TIP** **Recommendation**
>
> I recommend the following web page of my aromatics colleague, Andrea Stark: www.satureja.de.

Overall, some herbalist knowledge is very advisable as a specialist knowledge for distilling. Above all, this lets you look at all herbs in terms of their efficacy and aroma, and even any possible risk in case of overdosing if you did not already know this yourself. This herbalist knowledge helps you to evaluate hydrosols, as well as to make effective cosmetic products and remedies, and last but not least, to make your own liqueurs and schnapps.

> **TIP** **Recommendation**
>
> I am happy to recommend Peter Baumann's carefully composed website: www.kraeuter-verzeichnis.de.

Buy your supplies from a supplier you trust!

As a shopping source for ingredients and herbs, I would recommend finding a supplier in your area. In most larger cities you can find well-stocked herbal shops that provide expert advice. The supplier will also be happy to assist you in compiling good mixtures for specific ideas and purposes, and will be open to your distillation attempts. The same applies to fresh ingredients for distilling, first and foremost the live yeasts for making a mash of fresh fruit during the season. When buying live yeast cultures, make sure they are stored in an appropriately cool place. If the yeast is sitting in the sun in the shop window, you should not buy it; yeasts are temperature sensitive and can die at high temperatures. And it would certainly be annoying if your lovingly mashed specialty went bad because of the yeast. Ideally, yeasts should be stored in the refrigerator. The important thing is to trust your supplier. If you do not find a supplier near you, then order online. In essence, you can assume that the market has cleaned itself up and only "serious" suppliers remain. Pay attention to quality and reliability, and you can be sure that your supplies will reach you within a short time in the best fresh quality. Frequently deliveries from international suppliers are even fresher than those from small regional suppliers because of their faster goods turnover.

> **TIP** | **Recommendation**
>
> The following suppliers are probably the first choice for all general supplies for distillation. The third in the league is more specialized for beer brewing:
> www.destillatio.com
> www.holzeis.com
> www.brouwland.com

If you are looking for another still, the internet is certainly the best choice. I have tried to stay neutral in this book, and I recommend you look around on eBay and Amazon, but also at Destillatio.com, and compare the offers. You should balance what you have learned with your gut feeling and then buy the optimal still for you. If you are going to dive deeper into your new hobby of "distillation" any time soon, then you will decide sooner or later on getting a second still. You can also gladly try out one of the other options. If you are thinking about distilling privately using larger stills, I recommend you get a holiday cottage in Hungary. There private distilling is treated very generously, and you can buy a still with a capacity up to one hundred liters legally without registering with the authorities. I am happy to recommend a German-speaking supplier in Budapest at www.destillen-aus-ungarn.de.

In the end, I only have my book recommendations, some of which are in the area of distilling. I am very happy to recommend to you, as a supplement to this book, my book *Die hohe Kunst des Destillierens* (*The High Art of Distilling*, published by Stocker Verlag), which very extensively shows all the many possibilities for distilling. Especially for distilling essential oils, I recommend *Ätherische Öle selbst herstellen* (*Creating Essential Oils Yourself*), published by "Die Werkstatt" publishing house, which is the only book I know about distilling essential oils. On making hydrosols, I recommend *Hydrolate* (*Hydrosols*) by Ingrid Kleindienst-John, published by Freya Verlag. For the correct use and assessment of the efficacy of essential oils and hydrosols, I would use Eliane Zimmermann's *Aromatherapie: Die Heilkraft ätherischer Pfanzenöle* (*Aromatherapy: The Healing Power of Essential Plant Oils*), while the books by Susanne Fischer-Rizzi are absolutely worth reading. Try the wonderful *Das große Buch der Pfanzenwässer* (*The Big Book of Herbal Distillates*); you will be enthusiastic, and will surely find some new things that you might need when you are distilling. Unfortunately out of print and only rarely found in used bookshops for prices of up to $212 is the *Praktische Handbuch*

Further reading.

Create your own distilling book.

der Pfanzenalchemie (*Practical Handbook of Plant Chemistry*) by Manfred M. Junius. If you by chance are able to buy the book somewhere at a reasonable price then do it; this is a real treasure, with valuable hints on all kinds of different plant distillations, especially about making natural remedies and herbal essences.

If we now move on to making alcohol, it becomes somewhat more difficult in the legal area. Most of the books about distilling schnapps are directed at commercial distillers and have little to do with tabletop stills. Nevertheless, there is light on the horizon. I am glad to recommend, as a practical guide with many suggestions and recipes, *Schnapsbrennen als Hobby* (*Distilling Schnapps as a Hobby*), published by Werkstatt-Verlag: a book that every hobby distiller should have read and that goes into everything good about the two liter units that are legal in Austria. Leopold Stocker Verlag has also published *Whisky selbst gemacht* (*Home Made Whiskey*). Even more suitable for our purposes is *Handbuch für Whiskybrenner* (*Handbook for Whiskey Distillers*) by Dirk Gasser, because it deals exactly with our very small quantities and describes how you can distill genuine whiskey. Most of the other books refer to significantly larger quantities and are therefore rather uninteresting for our purposes. Concerning making mashes of different fruits, I could highly suggest *Von der Frucht zum Destillat* (*From Fruit to Distillate*) by Wilm Bartels. Even if it mostly deals with larger quantities, the book offers a very good overview.

Private distilleries are generally prohibited in Germany. This applies to all systems between 0.5 and 5 liters boiler volume.

Concluding Remarks

At this point I would like to thank my family, friends, and co-workers many times over.

If you have questions about distilling, do not be shy about asking me; I am happily available on Facebook. Alternatively, you may write me an email to frage@destillatio.com, which I will gladly answer.

Yours, Kai Möller

Have fun with all distillations!